Voices on the Wind

Voices on the Wind

Women Poets of the Celtic Twilight

Introduced and Edited by

Eilís Ní Dhuibhne

New Island Books / Dublin

Voices on the Wind
Women Poets of the Celtic Twilight
is first published in 1995 by
New Island Books,
2, Brookside,
Dundrum Road,
Dublin 14
Ireland

Introduction & Selection copyright ©
Eilís Ní Dhuibhne, 1995

ISBN 1 874597 23 5

New Island Books receives financial assistance from
The Arts Council (An Chomhairle Ealaíon),
Dublin, Ireland.

Cover design and painting of Susan Mitchell, Eva Gore-Booth
and Katharine Tynan by Jon Berkeley
Typeset by Graphic Resources
Printed in Ireland by Colour Books, Ltd.

Contents

2.   Susan Mitchell (1866 - 1926)

Introduction

The Irish Literary Revival, marking the birth of modern literature in Ireland in both the Irish and English languages, occurred in the last decades of the nineteenth century and the opening decade of the twentieth, although its seeds had been gestating slowly throughout most of the nineteenth century. The revival in Ireland was linked to the larger Celtic Literary Revival which was taking place in Brittany, Scotland and Wales, and to the liberal political movements promoting the ideal of small independent nations and initiating scholarly and artistic interest in minority, ethnic and popular cultures which had been taking place throughout Europe since the French Revolution. In Ireland, as in other parts of Europe, the literary and linguistic revivals were linked genetically to nationalist political developments, but this link was not necessarily manifest in the thought or work of many of the writers who belonged to the literary revival — being especially and interestingly ignored in the work of many of the women writers of the period.

The primary inspirations for the writers of the Revival were Old Irish literature and ancient mythology, contemporary folklore, and the customs and way of life of the country people, particularly those living in the western Irish-speaking regions. This vast body of imaginative material had been drawn upon earlier, by writers such as William Carleton and folklorists such as Patrick Kennedy and Crofton Croker, but the perception of it as something important intensified at the end of the nineteenth century, and a group of talented and committed writers, centred in Dublin — but maintaining links of various kinds with rural Ireland, particularly with the West — seized upon it as a source of imagery, energy, and stimulation. From this school of writers some of the most lasting and important poetry and drama of modern Anglo-Irish literature emerged, notably in the work of W.B. Yeats, John Millington Synge, and Lady Gregory.

There were many minor stars in the galaxy, however, some whose work was, in their early years, considered as promising as that of Yeats and who were, at the time, as important in energizing the Revival as any of those well-known writers whose works have better stood the test of time. A substantial proportion of the poets of the Revival were women, a fact which may seem surprising but in the historical context should not. The Revival was itself a product of the movements which were democratizing Europe and which embraced, as well as the ideals of nationalism and socialism, women's suffrage. The writers of the Revival were engaged in an exploration of the unofficial culture of Ireland, the stories, poems and myths of the small and marginalized people. It is not, in this context, surprising that the marginalized gender should have been given, or should have taken, a voice. Indeed, the prime mover of the theatrical revival was a women, Lady Gregory, and both Synge and Yeats were particularly interested in women, and not only as sexual companions or friends. Synge's admiration for an idealised type of strong independent woman—an Ibsenian superwoman, the ideal of the women's movement then and to some extent even now—is clearly manifest in his creation of characters such as Nora and Pegeen Mike. Yeats, possibly because of disillusioning experiences with real-life Noras, had more conservative ideals of femininity, but in practice was more feminist than anybody in his encouraging and helpful attitude to many women writers. His sense of the value of female experience as a subject for poetry was also astute. He wrote to Katharine Tynan, to whom he was a close friend and loyal and honest fellow-poet, following the publication of Tynan's last book of poetry, *Irish Poems* (1913): "I think you are at your best when you write as a mother and when you remember your old home and the Dublin mountains..." [Ann Connerton Fallon, *Katharine Tynan*, Boston, Twayne, 1979.]

Yeats' acceptance of personal female experiences, such as motherhood, as fit subject matter for poetry (actually on an equal footing with the Dublin mountains!), seems modern and even ahead of its time, as was Katharine Tynan's spontaneous and natural confidence in drawing on feminine experiences of many kinds for her work.

Katharine Tynan was a close friend of Yeats from his earliest years, and was a lively and enthusiastic member of the literary coterie which formed the nucleus of the Revival writers. Other women poets who belonged to the Irish Literary Revival were Susan Mitchell, Dora Sigerson Shorter, Ethna Carbery, Nora Hopper Chesson, and Eva Gore-Booth, and selections of their poems are included in this book.

The first quality which united these writers is an interest in Irish culture, and it is this quality which defines them as writers of the Literary Revival. Some of the poets, such as Katharine Tynan, and more particularly Eva Gore-Booth, wrote comparatively few poems which draw on the typical Celtic Twilight raw material of mythology and folklore, but they did draw on it occasionally and both wrote about the Irish landscape and way of life. Susan Mitchell's main concern with the

Celtic Twilight was to satirize it, and she is unique among these poets in writing comic verse or in displaying much sense of humour — wistfulness or sadness are the more predominant moods, as the titles of many of the poems and even the collections indicate, Nora Hopper Chesson's books, *Dirge for Aoine and Other Poems, A Dead Girl to Her Lover and Other Poems* and *The Waiting Widow and Other Poems* striking the keynote. Katharine Tynan's poems are, however, although never humorous, often happy in spirit. Dora Sigerson Shorter and Ethna Carbery wrote poems using exclusively "Celtic Twilight" themes, while the above mentioned Nora Hopper Chesson, called "the quintessence of what the public regarded as a Celtic Twilight poet — quietly charming and not unpleasantly vapid" in Robert Hogan's *A Dictionary of Irish Literature*, interspersed these with nature lyrics, and with poems based on motifs drawn from classical and Nordic mythology. It is perhaps worth noting that the last three poets, whose work did not develop as fully as that of Tynan, Mitchell or Gore-Booth, died relatively young: Hopper Chesson and Carbery in their early thirties and Dora Sigerson Shorter in her forties.

In general, the Celtic Twilight poems strike me as being less interesting than the other work written by the same poets. This is partly due to the fact that the same myths and stories —The Children of Lir, Diarmuid and Gráinne, Cúchulainn—tend to be used again and again, and have been explored by other writers since the period with which we are dealing. Such stories have become commonplace by now and are part and parcel of the schoolbook tradition, so that it is difficult to appreciate the freshness and novelty which they would have had in the 1890s. But for poets like Tynan or Hopper Chesson, these stories were exciting enough to be simply retold in verse. It was not considered necessary to question the meaning of the stories, to analyse them, or to relate them to personal or contemporary experience. Nor, apparently, did it occur to the poets of the Celtic Twilight that readers might benefit from being exposed more directly to the literature or mythology they used, through the medium of straightforward translations, for instance. Rather they perceived their task as the prettification and versification of the original stories, and presumably felt that they were more acceptable in these moulds than in anything more robust or primary. Like many other writers of the period, their mission, conscious or unconscious, was to transmit the primary literature and folklore of Gaelic Ireland to their readers in a diluted form.

It is important, in assessing the place of these poems in the history of Irish Literature, to try to understand the freshness of impact which they had at the time, although it is difficult to do this. It is also difficult to sympathise with the literary mood of the period in Ireland: the sturdy spirit of revolution and exploration which inspired the Literary Revival went hand in hand with many ridiculous sentiments relating to the nature of the so-called Celt. George Meredith, in his introduction to Dora Sigerson Shorter's *Collected Poems* (London 1907) described this tendency: "The mind of the Celt has been much discussed. It is generally taken to be overpoweringly emotional, vapourish as well, and fantastical, remote, divorced from reality." He goes on to make the sensible point that fantasy is usually a cloak for reality: "Symbolism swallows Reality, but Reality is read through it, if we take the trouble."

Not many of the poets of the Celtic Twilight appear to have taken the trouble to consider very deeply the relationship between the fantasies they used and the reality of the people who had originally created those fantasies, although occasionally, as in Katharine Tynan's "The Children of Lir", a very human sensitivity pervades the telling of the mythical tale. Indeed, the most important function of the Celtic material was one of inspiration and energizing. It provided these poets with themes, ideas and a cause at the start of their careers: the raw material was new — to them and their readers — significant, Irish, and readily available in a variety of secondary sources, thanks to the work of collectors and scholars throughout the nineteenth century. The stronger poets drew on this material initially or only intermittently. They then had the confidence or the need to write poetry that did not fit into the Celtic Twilight mould, but instead expressed their personal and individual imaginations and consciousness. These, rather than the poets who for one reason or another failed to move away from what was the fashion of the period, seem to me to be the better poets in this anthology.

I have presented examples of Celtic Twilight poems from all the poets included here, however, since it is important to acknowledge their role in this part of the Revival, and since this part of the repertoire of some of the writers, such as Tynan, indicates the great value of the traditional material in liberating the poets' imaginations and stimulating their linguistic and metaphorical skills. And sometimes, of course, these poems are quite striking *per se*. I have also included a wide selection drawn from the other, non-Celtic, poems of the various writers, with the intention of conveying an impression of the overall range of their work. As to its value, I think the poems speak for themselves. None of the poets represented in this anthology could claim to be a major poet, if an international standard is applied and if Yeats is taken as the yardstick of great poetry of the Irish Literary Revival. None had the intellectual, emotional, or artistic daring or adventurousness of Yeats. To that extent, they all missed the boat for Byzantium. But this is true for most of their contemporaries, many of whom have been naturally forgotten but some of whom are still acknowledged, for instance in the Field Day Anthology of Irish Literature. Within the ranks of minor poets of their period, some of the poets included here emerge as the more original and interesting voices: Katharine Tynan, Susan Mitchell and Eva Gore-Booth in particular are well-worth reassessing, and their work certainly serves to raise questions about the history of women's writing in Ireland.

For me, as a writer rather than a literary critic or scholar, there were many surprises in my exploration of this period. In the first place, the number of women writing and publishing poetry in Ireland at the turn of the century was something of a revelation, as was the sense which I have received from the contemporary commentaries on their work that it was thoroughly acceptable for women to write, that many of the foremost writers of the day, the male writers that is, encouraged and admired their female colleagues, that the best publishing houses published their work, and that there seems to have been no prejudice held against them by the literary establishment. (The badge "woman writer" was used, of course, which may in itself suggest that this initial impression is too rosy, and that there was a sense in which women were automatically relegated to a separate literary league, even by those who supported them.)

A second surprise was that themes which I have been used to considering as new and modern in poetry, for instance those related to domestic and suburban life and to motherhood and child rearing, occur with some frequency in the poetry of this period, directly in the work of Katharine Tynan and obliquely, filtered through folk legends and songs, in some of the other poets' verse. And a powerful feminist political consciousness is expressed with some spontaneity by Eva Gore-Booth. Less surprising, perhaps, is the impression that during the period in question Ireland was liberal and progressive, wide open to international influences in literary and intellectual matters at least, while at the same time boldly and adventurously obsessed with exploring and rediscovering Irish culture and identity. I feel that in this vigorous and eager atmosphere women's writing and self-expression was encouraged and allowed to flourish. By the year 1900 there were a number of what we now refer to as "role models" available to Irish women who wanted to write poems, plays or fiction. The question raised by this, by the writing and the writers presented in this anthology, is what happened next? Of course, some immensely gifted women in Ireland wrote in the decades between independence and the 1960s. But my impression is that they were few indeed, and that for some reason women in Ireland did not follow the pattern established during the Revival. Instead we have waited until the 1960s or 1970s to have another resurgence of writing by Irish women, a second literary revival.

The glib and simple answer to this question of what caused a paucity of women writers in those intervening years is "De Valera-ism". But the complex reason for the long hiatus is one which requires the attention of historians of literature and society. In the meantime, the poems and writers in this anthology are presented in the spirit of adventure and exploration which characterised their own personalities and the period during which they lived and wrote.

Eilís Ní Dhuibhne
Dublin, April 1995

Katharine Tynan
(1861 - 1931)

Katharine Tynan was born in Dublin and lived for the most of her youth in Clondalkin. In 1893 she married Henry Hinkson, a barrister, and moved to England, where their three children were born. The family returned to Ireland in 1911 and lived in Mayo. Henry Hinkson died in 1919, and following that Katharine Tynan made her living by writing.

Considered one of the most promising poets of the Irish Literary Revival, she was a close friend of W.B. Yeats, and received advice and encouragement from him throughout her life. Before her marriage, she was one of the central figures of Dublin's literary circle, and hosted weekly gatherings, on Sundays, at her father's farmhouse, which were attended by her friends — Yeats, Douglas Hyde, and George Russell among them.

Her first collection of poems, *Louise de La Valliere* was published at her father's expense in 1885, and was an immediate success. It was followed by the collections *Ballads and Lyrics* in 1891 and *A Lover's Breastknot* in 1896. These collections are usually regarded as her best, and I think the selection of poems presented here corroborates the general opinion. Although the later collections show a certain thematic expansion, insofar as the poems continue to reflect the changing experiences of the poet's life, their energy and vigour decline; in particular the language of the poems becomes thin.

Tynan, although a leading figure of the Literary Revival, did not write many poems on Celtic Twilight themes: "The Children of Lir"is one of these few. Included in her second collection, *Ballads and Lyrics*, it is one of her best poems in its use of language and nature imagery, and displays a striking and very unusual competence in dealing with the literary convention of anthropomorphization in a sophisticated way. Her swans manage to be convincing both as animals and humans, and the sentimentality which tinges this, as almost all her poems, is redeemed by imaginative and poetic vigour.

As I have previously stated, one of the functions which the Celtic Twilight themes served for the poets of the Literary Revival was to liberate and expand their imaginations, which could then progress to deal with more profound, personal and interesting matters. In "The Children of Lir", we see how this process is working for Katharine

Tynan, and several of the simpler poems, based on her own experience of love or religious feeling, for instance, in *Ballads and Lyrics* and *A Lover's Breastknot*, reveal the effects of the inspiration received, one supposes, from the old fantasies.

Her more mature work, however, seems to have lost its connection to the early source. The fantastic images, drawn from old literature or from nature, give way to banal language and metaphor. There are probably a number of reasons for this shift—it could be construed as an attempt by the poet to use a simple colloquial language, suited to her new range of subjects: love of children and husband, domesticity, gardening and other quotidian themes. But other less deliberate factors are no doubt involved. Katharine Tynan was an overly prolific writer, churning out hundreds of novels and also engaging regularly in journalistic writing and editorial work, as well as writing poems. It is thought that this constant production diluted the quality of her work. Her passionate poetic sensibility seems also to have diminished after her marriage. It is also possible that her move away from Yeats, after her marriage, literally distanced her from the poetic standard which he set. Her imagination dims and her poetry is less exciting in form and language, as she grows older. In terms of theme, however, it is very interesting. In her valuing of ordinary feminine concerns as fit matter for poems, she was revolutionary among Irish writers. I have included several of these domestic poems here, since my discovery of their existence served to revise my own view of the history of women's writing in Ireland, and I think they deserve to be known for their originality and spontaneity of thought, as well as for their simple attractiveness.

The Children of Lir

Out upon the sand-dunes thrive the coarse long grasses,
　　Herons standing knee-deep in the brackish pool,
Overhead the sunset fire and flame amasses,
　　And the moon to eastward rises pale and cool:
Rose and green around her, silver-grey and pearly,
　　Chequered with the black rooks flying home to bed;
For, to wake at daybreak, birds must couch them early,
　　And the day's a long one since the dawn was red.

On the chilly lakelet, in that pleasant gloaming,
　　See the sad swans sailing: they shall have no rest:
Never a voice to greet them save the bittern's booming
　　Where the ghostly sallows sway against the West.
"Sister," saith the grey swan, "Sister, I am weary,"
　　Turning to the white swan wet, despairing eyes;
"O," she saith, "my young one. O," she saith, "my dearie,"
　　Casts her wings about him with a storm of cries.

Woe for Lir's sweet children whom their vile stepmother
　　Glamoured with her witch-spell for a thousand years;
Died their father raving, on his throne another,
　　Blind before the end came from the burning tears.
Long the swans have wandered over lake and river.
　　Gone is all the glory of the race of Lir,
Gone and long forgotten like a dream of fever;
　　But the swans remember the sweet days that were.

Hugh, the black and white swan with the beauteous feathers,
　　Fiachra, the black swan with the emerald breast,
Conn, the youngest, dearest, sheltered in all weathers,
　　Him his snow-white sister loves the tenderest.
These her mother gave her as she lay a-dying

To her faithful keeping; faithful hath she been,
With her wings spread o'er them when the tempest's crying,
    And her songs so hopeful when the sky's serene.

Other swans have nests made 'mid the reeds and rushes,
    Lined with downy feathers where the cygnets sleep
Dreaming, if a bird dreams, till the daylight blushes,
    Then they sail out swiftly on the current deep.
With the proud swan-father, tall, and strong, and stately,
    And the mild swan-mother, grave with household cares,
All well-born and comely, all rejoicing greatly:
    Full of honest pleasure is a life like theirs.

But alas! for my swans, with the human nature,
    Sick with human longings, starved for human ties,
With their hearts all human cramped to a bird's stature,
    And the human weeping in the bird's soft eyes,
Never shall my swans build nests in some green river,
    Never fly to Southward in the autumn grey,
Bear no tender children, love no mates for ever,
    Robbed alike of bird's joys and of man's are they.

Babbles Conn the youngest, "Sister, I remember
    At my father's palace how I went in silk,
Ate the juicy deer-flesh roasted from the ember,
    Drank from golden goblets my child's draught of milk.
Once I rode a-hunting, laughed to see the hurly,
    Shouted at the ball-play, on the lake did row;
You had for your beauty gauds that shone so rarely."
    "Peace," saith Fionnuala, "that was long ago."

"Sister," saith Fiachra, "well do I remember
    How the flaming torches lit the banquet-hall
And the fire leapt skyward in the mid-December,

And among the rushes slept our stag-hounds tall.
By our father's right hand you sat shyly gazing,
    Smiling half and sighing, with your eyes aglow,
As the bards sang loudly, all your beauty praising."
    "Peace," saith Fionnuala, "that was long ago."

"Sister," then saith Hugh, "most do I remember
    One I called my brother, one, earth's goodliest man,
Strong as forest oaks are where the wild vines clamber,
    First at feast or hunting, in the battle's van.
Angus, you were handsome, wise and true, and tender,
    Loved by every comrade, feared by every foe:
Low, low, lies your beauty, all forgot your splendour."
    "Peace," saith Fionnuala, "that was long ago."

Dews are in the clear air, and the roselight paling,
    Over sands and sedges shines the evening star,
And the moon's disc lonely high in heaven is sailing,
    Silvered all the spear-heads of the rushes are,—
Housèd warm are all things as the night grows colder,
    Water-fowl and sky-fowl dreamless in the nest;
But the swans go drifting, drooping wing and shoulder
    Cleaving the still water where the fishes rest.

The Blackbird

(A new song with an old burden.)

There's a lark in the noon sky, a thrush on the tree,
And a linnet sings wildly across the green lea,
And the finches are merry, the cuckoos still call,
But where is my Blackbird, the dearest of all?

They may talk of their gold-crests, but if he were by,
With his hair like the velvet and liquid dark eye,
What yellow-haired Saxon or Dane might compare
With my honey-voiced Blackbird, and the night on his hair?

There were many would love him, with beauty and wealth;
At the dance and the hurley, love-looks went by stealth
From blue eyes and brown eyes: he saw only me.
God bless my bold Blackbird, wherever he be.

When I went out a-walking the fields were all green,
With a wide drift of sunshine, and daisies between,
And the birds sang at building, but tears made me blind
For my Blackbird of April, so handsome and kind.

Oh, if we were building our nest, I and he,
With my voice for his pleasure, and his song for me,
I would sing all the summer, and make the birds mad,
For the love of my Blackbird, the one love I had!

Over Mountains

My heart went roaming and flying
    Where her one treasure was.
The East was luridly dying,
    A low wind sobbed, "Alas!"

There was no bird at all
    Out of its nest so warm:
Over the mountain wall
    My heart went into storm.

And when the night was mirk,
    And on the shrieking sea
The wind was doing its work,
    My heart came back to me.

Tapped at my window-pane.
    Out of the storm and din,
Out of the night and rain,
    I rose and let her in.

O, heart, like a frightened bird,
    Heart like a small grey dove,
Say hast thou seen or heard
    Anything of our love?

But never a word she said,
    Her eye was leaden and dim,
Her breast had a stain of red,
    She spake no word of him.

And whether she saw him not
    Over the mountains grey,
Or whether he had forgot,
    I know not to this day.

House-Building

I've heard the mellow blackbird singing clearly
    Over the building of his wattled house,
Wherein some morn, when skies are rose and pearly,
    A small brown head shall bend to hear his vows.

I've seen the merry squirrel hoard his treasure
    Of milk-white nuts against a time of cold:
The little mate who shares his simple pleasure
    Hath eyes of amber and a fur of gold.

Oh, happy creatures, sweet is the providing,
    Sweet is the building of the little home!
Oh, sweet, I know, to gather up in hiding
    Treasures to deck the rooms where love shall come.

The light heart makes the hard work sweet and easy.
    Sweet is the time when all the world grows green,
And love puts off his splendours and is busy
    Building the house and decking it within.

A Woman

As one might see an enchanted land
Mistily over sea and strand
Purple and gold on the sky-line,
And since he might not go would pine,
So is she, with her old joys dead,
Her rose of life all witherèd.

Nay, there is ripe gold on the wheat,
And the wind bids you welcome, sweet.
Are lilies in the garden bed,
And a lark singing overhead,
Mists of blue Summer, and aloft,
Ripe apples in the orchard croft.

She will not hear. She sees across
The world, with a sick sense of loss,
A house that none hath builded well,
A heaven wherein she shall not dwell,
A threshold that she may not pass.
Hearth-fires that none hath lit, alas!

Voices of children calling her
Mother, to make her heart-strings stir,
Are calling in that lonely house;
Sweet as young birds the dawn will rouse,
The yellow heads against her knee
Flutter and dance untiringly.

And since one man will never come
And take her hand and lead her home
Opening the long-locked door for her,
The glory withers off the year,
Though she is patient: but to-day
Life goes for her a dusty way.

And for that music more forlorn,
Voices of children never born,
And the love words that are not hers,
Even the sweet sky choristers
Pleasure her not. Oh, let her be,
She and her dreams are company.

Only in August

Only in August I have not seen you.
    August comes with his wheat and poppies;
    Ruddy sunlight in corn and coppice;
Only in August I have not seen you.

Autumn beckons far-off like a greeting.
    I and Autumn have secrets of you,
    All the Winter was long to love you;
Wintry winds have a song of meeting.

Dear is Summer, but Spring is dearer.
    In the Spring there was heavenly weather;
    Love and sunshine and you together.
Dear is Summer, but Spring is dearer.

June is fled with her rose and pansies.
    More is gone than a drift of roses,
    More than the may that the May uncloses,
More than April-with songs and dances.

Only in August I have not seen you.
    Every month hath its share of graces,
    Flowers, and song, and beloved faces.
Only in August I have not seen you.

Sheep and Lambs

All in the April evening,
    April airs were abroad,
The sheep with their little lambs
    Passed me by on the road.

The sheep with their little lambs
    Passed me by on the road;
All in the April evening
    I thought on the Lamb of God.

The lambs were weary, and crying
    With a weak, human cry.
I thought on the Lamb of God
    Going meekly to die.

Up in the blue, blue mountains
    Dewy pastures are sweet
Rest for the little bodies,
    Rest for the little feet.

But for the Lamb of God,
    Up on the hill-top green,
Only a Cross of shame
    Two stark crosses between.

All in the April evening,
    April airs were abroad,
I saw the sheep with their lambs,
    And thought on the Lamb of God.

Green Gravel

A CHILD'S RHYME

Green gravel! green gravel! the grass is so green
For the prettiest young fair maid that ever was seen.
We'll wash her in new-milk, and clothe her in pink,
And write down her name with a gold pen and ink.

Her eyes are like diamonds, her hair is like wheat,
And her cheeks like the roses so dainty and sweet;
She'll have gowns of the velvet, and a gay golden comb,
And a ring on her finger, when her true love comes home.

Green gravel! green gravel! your true love sends word
That he dons all his bravest and buckles on his sword,
And is coming to wed you, so preen you up fine,
Set the music a-going, and flowing the wine.

Now he comes for to marry her, we'll dress her in white,
Sprinkled over with daisies so golden and bright,
And a veil of fine silver we'll throw on her hair,
Lest the roses grow envious and die of despair.

But where is he tarrying, the gallant bridegroom?
For the priest's in the parlour, and the bride in her room.
And the bridesmaids have left her to sigh her soft sigh,
To her tears, and her smiling, and her mother's goodbye.

Green gravel! green gravel! your true love is dead,
And he sends you a message to turn round your head;
And to turn on your pillow with your face to the wall,
You're a maid and a widow and no wife at all!

Cold, cold in her bride-clothes she lay down so meek,
With her hands on her bosom and her hair by her cheek;
Now come, ye fine gentlemen, and bear ye the bride
Where her bridegroom is sleeping. Let them sleep side by
    side!

From LOVE'S SUMMER:

II

Summer Sweet

Honey-Sweet, sweet as honey smell the lilies,
    Little lilies of the gold in a ring;
Little censers of pale gold are the lilies,
    That the wind, sweet and sunny, sets a-swing.

Smell the rose, sweet of sweets, all a-blowing!
    Hear the cuckoo call in dreams, low and sweet!
Like a very John-a-Dreams coming, going.
    There's honey in the grass at our feet.

There's honey in the leaf and the blossom,
    And honey in the night and the day.
And honey-sweet the heart in Love's bosom,
    And honey-sweet the words Love will say.

From LOVE'S SUMMER:

III

Sounds

Bees in the white and scarlet cell
    Of bean-flowers and in beds of thyme;
The leader of the sheep his bell
    Ringeth my even-song and prime;
He leads his flock at morning early
    Out to the dark grass sewn with gold,
And when the evening dews are pearly,
    Back to the fold.

Somewhere they mow the grass: the sound
    Brings with it fresh and fragrant breaths.
And little airs all scent be-drowned,
    Blown from the white and purple heaths.
The last bird sings his waning passion.
    And you, whose love can never fail,
Take up the burden and narration
    Of the sweet tale.

From LOVE'S SUMMER:

I V

August Weather

Dead heat and windless air,
    And silence over all;
Never a leaf astir,
    But the ripe apples fall;
Plums are purple-red,
    Pears amber and brown;
Thud! in the garden-bed
    Ripe apples fall down.

Air like a cider press
    With the bruised apples' scent;
Low whistles express
    Some sleepy bird's content;
Still world and windless sky,
    A mist of heat o'er all;
Peace like a lullaby,
    And the ripe apples fall.

The Mother

Great passions I awake that must
Bow any woman to the dust
With fear lest she should fail to rise
As high as those enamoured eyes.

Now for those flying days and sweet
I sit in Beauty's Mercy-Seat.
My smiles, my favours I award,
Since I am beautiful, adored.

They praise my cheeks, my lips my eyes,
With Love's most exquisite flatteries,
Covet my hands that they may kiss
And to their ardent bosoms press.

My foot upon the nursery stair
Makes them a music rich and rare;
My skirt that rustles as I come
For very rapture strikes them dumb.

What jealousies of word and glance!
The light of my poor countenance
Lights up their world that else were drear.
"But you are lovely, mother dear!"

I go not to my grave but I
Know Beauty's full supremacy:
Like Cleopatra's self, I prove
The very heights and depths of Love.

So to be loved, so to be wooed,
Oh, more than mortal woman should!
What if she fail or fall behind!
Lord, make me worthy, keep them blind!

The Meeting

As I went up and he came down, my little six-year boy,
Upon the stairs we met and kissed, I and my tender Joy.
O fond and true, as lovers do, we kissed and clasped and
    parted;
And I went up and he went down, refreshed and
    happy-hearted.

What need was there for any words, his face against my
    face?
And in the silence heart to heart spoke for a little space
Of tender things and thoughts on wings and secrets none
    discovers;
And I went up and he went down, a pair of happy lovers.

His clinging arms about my neck, what need was there for
    words?
O little heart that beat so fast like any fluttering bird's!
"I love," his silence said; "I love," my silence answered
    duly;
And I went up and he went down comforted
    wonderfully.

The New Boy

He never knew before how heavenly the places,
   Light-loved but yesterday, the fields of his home;
Gleam to his sick eyes the lost belovèd faces,
   A mirage, a water-well, where he may not come.

Dear was the white road, winding and turning,
   Where his free feet ran nor knew them free.
Beacons the low house, a heaven to his yearning,
   A heaven of accustomed things where he may not be.

Round the smooth cricket ground the woods, a watch
      keeping,
   Draw a dark barrier where he may not pass.
What is work? What is play? The sad hours go creeping.
   His heaven's out of reach, and none cares, alas!

His tears make a water-course; his poor cheeks grimy;
   His heart hangs so heavy and his feet are lead.
Oh, what to him is *Audio*? And what is *Eime*?
   Who only wants his mother's breast for his aching head.

Boys alike and masters, phantoms to his vision.
   The high class-room walls the cage to the bird.
He heeds not the chill kindness nor the sly derision,
   Sick for his mother's kiss, his father's word.

Far, far away, beyond those drear spaces,
   Beyond the sullen hours that creep away,
Lie the deliverance, the heavenly places.
   He strangles with his sobs till the grey day.

Planting Bulbs

Setting my bulbs arow
    In cold earth under the grasses,
Till the frost and the snow
    Are gone and the Winter passes —

Sudden a foot-fall light,
    Sudden a bird-call ringing;
And these in gold and in white
    Shall rise with a sound of winging;

Airy and delicate all,
    All go trooping and dancing
At Spring's call and foot-fall,
    Airily dancing, advancing.

In the dark of the year,
    Turning the earth so chilly,
I look to the day of cheer,
    Primrose and daffodilly.

Turning the sods and the clay,
    I think on the poor sad people
Hiding their dead away
    In the churchyard, under the steeple.

All poor women and men,
    Broken-hearted and weeping,
Their dead they call on in vain,
    Quietly smiling and sleeping.

Friends, now listen and hear,
    Give over crying and grieving,
There shall come a day and a year
    When the dead shall be as the living.

There shall come a call, a foot-fall,
    And the golden trumpeters blowing
Shall stir the dead with their call,
    Bid them be rising and going.

Then in the daffodil weather
    Lover shall run to lover;
Friends all trooping together;
    Death and Winter be over.

Laying my bulbs in the dark,
    Visions have I of hereafter.
Lip to lip, breast to breast, hark!
    No more weeping, but laughter.

The Little Hill

There's a little hill, a round green hill, in my own country;
And shaped like a little breast it is, so round to see;
O, shaped like a little breast it is, so smooth, so mild.
The milky breast of the earth it is, warm for the child.

There's a little hill and a hundred streams flow down its
    side.
And I would that I might creep there now, creep there and
    hide,
And drink my fill of the honeyed milk, drink and be full,
And the thirst of the heart be quenched in me in the
    shadows cool!

There's never a day of the hottest days but you'd find there
    yet
The plash of the water under your feet and a fragrance wet;
And the water-weeds they stand to their knees in the
    emerald flow;
And the silver fin of a trout'll be in the pool below.

There's a blackbird, too, in the dusk and dew and he sings a
    strain
Must draw the ache from the weary heart and the fever
    pain.
Sure he'll sing his song all the evening long full of trouble
    and joy —
The honeyed note and the golden throat and the heart of a
    boy.

To that little hill in my own country if I might come
And lie at rest on that milky breast in the fields at
    home!
There's dust in my heart and dust in my throat, and I
    crying still
For the song I knew in the dusk and dew and the little
    green hill.

Cowslips

The children run and leap
   By a most heavenly hill.
And I will give you the Keys of Heaven
   To use as you will.

The keys are small and sweet;
   Gold keys from a girdle swung;
The cowslip opens the Gates of Heaven
   To the pure and the young.

The children are gold and white-
   Gold heads the mothers have kissed;
The children carry the Keys of Heaven
   Swung at the wrist.

Children, why would ye go?
   Here is a heavenly land.
The children swinging the Keys of Heaven
   Slip from your hand.

Is it not Heaven enough
   Here for a little while?
The children kissing the Keys of Heaven
   Listen and smile.

The children are white as snow;
   They walk in gold to their knees;
The children who hold the Keys of Heaven
   Go where they please.

Maternity

There is no height, no depth, my own, could set us apart,
Body of mine and soul of mine: heart of my heart!

There is no sea so deep, my own, no mountain so high,
That I should not come to you if I heard you cry.

There is no hell so sunken, no heaven so steep,
Where I should not seek my own, find you and keep.

Now you are round and soft to see, sweet as a rose,
Not a stain on my spotless one, white as the snows.

If some day you came to me heavy with sin,
I, your mother, would run to the door and let you in.

I would wash you white again with my tears and grief,
Body of mine and soul of mine, till you found relief.

Though you had sinned all sins there are 'twixt east and
   west,
You should find my arms wide for you, your head on
   my breast.

Child, if I were in heaven one day and you were in hell —
Angels white as my spotless one stumbled and fell —

I would leave for you the fields of God and Queen Mary's
   feet,
Straight to the heart of hell would go, seeking my sweet.

God mayhap would turn Him around at sound of the door:
Who is it goes out from Me to come back no more?

Then the blessed Mother of God would say from her throne:
Son, 'tis a mother goes to hell, seeking her own.

Body of mine, and soul of mine, born of me,
Thou who wert once little Jesus beside my knee.

It is like to that all mothers are made: Thou madest them so.
Body of mine and soul of mine, do I not know?

Shanganagh

To Mrs. Rowan Hamilton

Laughs the darling river, hurrying, dancing onward.
 Sorrows she knows of maybe, the bird's or the bee's,
Or some butterfly weary, its wings dropped downward,
 Caught in a swirling eddy, drowned in her seas.

Maybe the hedge-sparrow, maybe the starling,
 Hath lost here some sweet thing of its downy brood.
Never lamb or kid or any woman's darling
 Hath she thought of drowning in her wildest mood.

From her golden bed, set with many a jewel,
 No white face starts upward, piteous to the skies;
None hath sought here rest from sweet love grown cruel,
 Hiding a sad secret from the mocking eyes.

Bare she lies to Heaven 'mid her mints and cresses,
 Innocent of evil as a lamb or a child.
The sun and stars love her and the wing caresses,
 Ruffling her little waters so soft and wild.

As she slips away by a mossy boulder
 The child dips a rosy foot where she foams and swirls,
Shows her a darling cheek and a dimpled shoulder,
 Laughs to see his face in her, set in its curls.

Here the lamb drinks deep without fear or fretting:
 There are no wolves, no danger, for child or lamb:
Only the Angels of God that are never forgetting
 Keep the child for his mother, the lamb for his dam.

The Little House

To Alice Meynell

I will have a little house
    When the children are flown.
The feel of a big house
    Would be cold as a stone;
A house full of emptiness
    And we two alone.

But in a little house
    We could creep to the blaze;
We could warm our old hearts
    With the thought of old days;
Him and me together
    When the firelight plays.

There would hardly be room
    For the ghosts to come in:
Ghosts of the little children
    Who made a merry din,
Long ago and long ago
    When I was a queen.

I will have a little garden
    Big enough for two,
Where we can walk together
    When the skies are blue,
Talking the good days over
    And how fast they flew.

The littlest house and garden
    For him and me just.
And all the sweet times we had
    Withered to dust.
A big house would break my heart
    For the children lost.

Gorse

To W.B. Yeats who taught me.

Many a year I loved the gorse on an English common,
    Miles on miles of the golden cups and the nutty wine,
Cloth of gold for the tramping folk, poor men and women;
    Still my heart said in complaint: It is not mine.

Here's a golden wall each side the hill we're breasting;
    Never sure was the English gorse as great as this!
Grapes of gold from a golden vine for the wild bees'
        questing;
    A world of gold and a pearly cloud on a blue abyss.

There's a golden hill behind us now, gold on the azure,
    The dearest hill like a little breast in gold above.
The lark springs from a golden bed, spilling his treasure
    Down on the buttercup fields of light and his hidden
        love.

Over the hill we bathe our feet in golden water,
    A little steam the traveller fords, so clear and cold.
But is it May of the leafing—the High King's daughter
    For all her green is under the wave of the flooding gold.

Over the hill — the yellow hill, the Spears are showing,
    The Silver Spears are turned to gold o'er the valley's
        haze.
There's a small gold shower on the mountain now and the
river flowing
    Flows in and out like a ribbon of gold through the Milky
        Ways.

The eager bees plunge to the thighs in a brimming chalice,
　　Their bag so full of the golden spoils they scarce can
　　　　fly —
The mountain calls to the mountain now, over the valleys,
　　"Friend, we are Kings in the house of Kings, you
　　　　and I."

Here with a heart fed of delight as a bee with honey
　　I sit like a miser counting the gold, nor shall repine,
For the cuckoo's roaming the golden street, blithesome
　　and bonny —
　　My heart says to my heart: Have peace: this
　　beauty's thine.

Haymaking

In Connaught, 1915

Aye, sure, it does always be rainin'
    An' the hay lyin' out in the wet,
But what's the good o' complainin'?
    It never made things better yet!
There'll be musty hay in the manger,
    The cow's goin' dry, be mischance,
And the boy that went for a Ranger
    Is lost on us-somewhere in France!

The father of him, it's heart-breakin' —
    Wid a watery glint o' the sun,
It's out wid him, turnin' an' shakin' —
    Then all the labour's undone.
There won't be much savin' in Connaught,
    The winter'll be hungry and black,
But I wouldn't waste sorrow upon it
    If only the boy could come back!

There's a terrible cloud over Nephin,
    An' the rain rushin' up from the say,
Och, what if the hay is past savin'?
    I wouldn't be mindin' the hay.
'Tis the loss of the boy's bent me double,
    An' the poor ould man is as bad;
I'm starvin' for him, an' the trouble,
    The trouble's heavy and sad.

God's good and He'll send better weather,
    The sun'll be shinin' again,
If Pat and me was together
    I wouldn't be mindin' the rain.
No matter what weather was in it
    I wouldn't care if he'd come.
But the heart o' me's cryin' this minit,
    For the boy that'll never come home!

The Long Vacation

To Amy Wainwright

This is the time the boys come home from school,
    Filling the house with gay and happy noise,
Never at rest from morn till evening cool —
    All the roads of the world bring home the boys.

This is the time — but still they are not come;
    The mothers stand in the doorway listening long;
Long, long they shall wait ere the boys come home.
    Where do they tarry, the dear, the light-heart throng?

Their feet are heavy as lead and deep their rest.
    The mothers watch the road till set of sun;
But nevermore the birds fly back to the nest.
    The roads of the world run Heavenward every one.

High Summer

Pinks and syringa in the garden closes
And the sweet privet hedge and golden roses.
The pines hot in the sun, the drone of the bee;
They die in Flanders to keep these for me.

The long sunny days and the still weather,
The cuckoo and the blackbird shouting together,
The lambs calling their mothers out on the lea;
They die in Flanders to keep these for me.

The doors and windows open: South wind blowing
Warm through the clean sweet rooms, on tip-toe going,
Where many sanctities, dear and delightsome be —
They die in Flanders to keep these for me.

Daisies leaping in foam on the green grasses,
The dappled sky and the stream that sings as it passes —
These are bought with a price, a bitter fee —
They die in Flanders to keep these for me.

The Vision of Mary

There's a white rose on the thorn,
    A red rose on the tree,
And Christ is born on Christmas morn
    That all men may go free.

The white rose for Mary,
    The red rose for her Son;
When she came down through the sleeping town,
    The red and white were one.

Curled like a little moon
    He shone amid the hay,
The stars forsake their heavenly track
    To sing him lullalay.

She kneels for to adore
    The earth and Heaven's Desire.
Oh, what is this beneath her kiss
    Throbs like a little fire?

In each small hand she sees
    A red rose-petal lie,
And while she sees hath little ease
    Lest Herod should draw nigh.

And when on each small foot
    She sees the red-rose stain,
She would snatch him fast unto her breast
    Lest he in snares be ta'en.

Oh, when she sees the smirch
    Of the red rose on His side,
What sword is in her heart; what dart
    That will not be denied?

What coronal of gems,
    Of ruby or coral spine,
Now, now is laid on His pretty head,
    With His sweet curls doth twine?

His Mother stoops to kiss
    The wounds of her Baby Son;
In dreams she sees a high trellis
    And one red rose thereon.

The sword turns in her heart,
    She clasps Him warm and close,
With lullaby-loo His fret unto
    She lulls her Destined Rose.

The Grey Country

I dreamt a dream on November Night
    Of the dear souls that wait in pain
For the full vision, the Delight,
    Beauty that shall not change nor wane.

The grey country's to Heaven close,
    Not Heaven but almost Heaven's twin;
As a grey rose to a gold rose,
    As a grey image faint and thin.

In the grey land were bliss enough
    Did not the Vision shine and gleam,
Turning the softest way to rough
    Until they might attain to Him.

Mary walking in Heaven's bower
    Heard the sighing after her Son:
Give me Thy Mercy for an hour,
    Thou who wert once my little one!

Mary came with stars in her hair,
    The new moon was under her feet;
In the grey world so still and fair
    The heart of the world began to beat.

Some were clinging beside her skirt,
    Soul on soul like a flock of birds;
Others nested, oh, past desert!
    On the heart that had seven swords.

Mary gathers them one and all,
    Many a one late home from war,
As they were children tender and small —
    Sweetly gathers them all to her.

As a green tree in the birds' flight
    I saw Mary amid her flock,
Carrying souls in her veil white,
    Hiding them warm in her blue cloak.

The Grey Mornings

The grey mornings I well remember,
The grey mountains new-waked from slumber,
The grey dews on the trees and hedges,
And in grey distance the grey sea's edges.

Cool it was, sweet beyond telling,
The grey-green hay in the pastures smelling,
The grey meadows wet as a river,
The grey dew where the grass-blades quiver.

Grey gulls and the sea-grey swallow
Take the track that my heart would follow.
Home from the heat and the cruel weather,
That I and my heart might fare together!

Purple-grey are the wild hills showing,
Silver-grey is the west wind blowing.
O grey fields and grey hills behind you,
Would my feet might follow and find you!

The Silent Time

Singing of birds is over: the Curlew only
    Out by the bog-pools bids his mate to beware.
Long sweet whistles under the rushes lonely
    Set to listen the dew-wet ears of a hare.

Ears and eyes that turn backward. Only the plover
    Pipes and is silent; the singing of birds is done:
Over the marriage-song and the song of a lover;
    Over the songs to the children feathered and flown.

The wood-dove hidden in leafage mourning for ever,
    Because her children are Two, only Two, only Two,
And the Wren and the Robin have Nine and Ten in the
      quiver.
    What will she do, the soft Wood-dove? What will she
    do?

The Curlew calls love-calls and his mate will listen,
    The Wood-dove mourns and mourns and is never still.
The hare hears; the dew on his ears a-glisten;
    He thinks it a whistling boy coming over the hill.

The House Of Life

The life of the body's a cage,
    And the soul within it
Frets to escape, to be free,
    Like a lark or a linnet.
But since the struggle's in vain,
    She is weary ere long;
She chirps and she sings a little
    To assuage her wrong.

Behind the bars she sits brooding
    Her evil mishap,
Like a wild little hare or a rabbit
    That's caught in a trap,
Till, dazed with despair, she is weary,
    And struggles no more,
But plays with the sun and leaf-shadow
    That dance on the floor.

They call-they call to each other;
    O sister so small,
Are you there? Are you there, little brother,
    Behind the blank wall?
Like a bird, or a hare, or a rabbit,
    Frightened, undone,
The soul calls to another,
    That she be not alone.

The Old Country

As I go home at end of day, the old road,
Through the enchanted country full of my dreams,
By the dim hills, under the pellucid o'er-arching sky,
Home to the West, full of great clouds and the sunset,
Past the cattle that stand in rich grass to the knees,
It is not I who go home: it is not I.

Here is the turn we took, going home with my father,
The little feet of the pony trotting fast,
Home by the winding lane full of music of water,
He and I, we were enough for each other;
Going home through the silver, the pearly twilight,
I content with my father, he with his daughter.

Magical country, full of memories and dreams,
My youth lies in the crevices of your hills;
Here in the silk of your grass by the edge of the meadows,
Every flower and leaf has its memories of you.
Home was home then and the people friendly,
And you and I going home in the lengthening shadows.

Now I go home no more, though the swift car glides,
Carries me fast through the dear, the heavenly country.
No one knows me, the cottages show strange faces,
They who were kindly, who bid me "God save You!"
    of yore,
They are gone, they are flown, and only the country's
    the same,
And you sleeping so quietly under the grass.

The Choice

When skies are blue and days are bright
A kitchen-garden's my delight,
Set round with rows of decent box
And blowsy girls of hollyhocks.

Before the lark his Lauds hath done
And ere the corncrake's southward gone;
Before the thrush good-night hath said
And the young Summer's put to bed.

The currant-bushes' spicy smell,
Homely and honest, likes me well.
The while on strawberries I feast,
And raspberries the sun hath kissed.

Beans all a-blowing by a row
Of hives that great with honey go,
With mignonette and heaths to yield
The plundering bee his honey-field.

Sweet herbs in plenty, blue borage
And the delicious mint and sage,
Rosemary, marjoram, and rue,
And thyme to scent the winter through.

Here are small apples growing round,
And apricots all golden-gowned,
And plums that presently will flush
And show their bush a Burning Bush.

Cherries in nets against the wall,
Where Master Thrush his madrigal
Sings, and makes oath, a churl is he
Who grudges cherries for a fee.

Lavender, sweet-briar, orris. Here
Shall Beauty make her pomander,
Her sweet balls for to lay in clothes
That wrap her as the leaves the rose.

Take roses red and lilies white,
A kitchen-garden's my delight;
Its gillyflowers and phlox and cloves,
And its tall cote of irised doves.

Larks

All day in exquisite air
The song clomb an invisible stair,
Flight on flight, story on story,
Into the dazzling glory.

There was no bird, only a singing,
Up in the glory, climbing and winging,
Like a small golden cloud at even,
Trembling 'twixt earth and heaven.

I saw no staircase, winding, winding,
Up in the dazzle, sapphire and blinding,
Yet round by round, in exquisite air,
The song went up the stair.

Any Woman

I am the pillars of the house;
    The keystone of the arch am I.
Take me away, and roof and wall
    Would fall to ruin utterly.

I am the fire upon the hearth,
    I am the light of the good sun,
I am the heat that warms the earth,
    Which else were colder than a stone.

At me the children warm their hands;
    I am their light of love alive.
Without me cold the hearthstone stands,
    Nor could the precious children thrive.

I am the twist that holds together
    The children in its sacred ring,
Their knot of love, from whose close tether
    No lost child goes a-wandering.

I am the house from floor to roof,
    I deck the walls, the board I spread;
I spin the curtains, warp and woof,
    And shake the down to be their bed.

I am their wall against all danger,
    Their door against the wind and snow.
Thou Whom a woman laid in manger,
    Take me not till the children grow!

Susan Mitchell
(1866 - 1926)

Susan Mitchell was born in Carrick-on-Shannon, and lived in London and Dublin. She was assistant editor to George Russell on the magazine *The Irish Homestead* from 1901 onwards. She wrote a few volumes of serious poems, dealing with love, loss, and religious sentiment. Her most memorable work is her humorous verse, however, particularly that included in the volume *Aids to the Immortality of Certain Persons in Dublin: Charitably Administered*, from which most of the poems reproduced here are drawn. The book includes satirical poems on the Abbey, Yeats and Synge, and Irish politicians on both the Nationalist and Unionist sides. A favourite butt is George Russell, her boss. While some of the jokes are rather 'in house' and consequently no longer wildly amusing, quite a few of them are still effective enough. One of the most humorous parts of *Aids to the Immortality of Certain Persons* is the author's introduction, in which she, like many writers before her, anticipates the reviewer's response: "For the writer with no critical faculty, the ordinary commercial reviewer may be good enough, but when one is exceptionally gifted, as I am, with both the critical and creative faculty, why should he wait for any middle interest, like reviewing, to wriggle in between him and his victim the public...?"

Oh No!
We Never Mention It!

(Air: Early Victorian)

['This play (*The Playboy of the Western World*), in which one
of the characters makes use of a word that no refined woman
would mention, even to herself.' — Writer in the *Freeman*.]

Oh no, we never mention it, its name is never heard —
New Ireland sets its face against the once familiar word.
They take me to the Gaelic League where men wear kilts,
    and yet
The simple word of childhood's days I'm bidden to forget!

They tell me no one says it now, but yet to give me ease —
If I must speak they bid me use a word that rhymes
    with 'sneeze'.
But oh! their cold-permission my spirits cannot lift —
I only want the dear old word, the one that ends in 'ift.'

O cruel Gaelic Leaguers! cruel Sinn Feiners all!
Have you no little sisters, who once when very small,
Before they knew what sinfulness could lurk in one
    wee word —
Have you not from their artless lips its simple accents heard?

Then by those early memories, hearken to one who prays
The right to mention once again the word of other days,
Without police protection once more her voice to lift —
The right to tell (even to herself) that still she wears —a shift!

The Cabinet Council—
A Suppressed Letter

To Birrell spake Sir Edward Grey:
   'Our good friend Theodore
To Plunkett doth a tribute pay
By letter unto us to-day.'
   Said Birrell, 'What a bore!'

'Nay, be not nervous, Birrell, though
   We men in office dread
The postman's knock, for well we know
It has rained many a knock-down blow
   On many a wooden head.

'These are good words that Roosevelt sends,
   And real glad I am;
This letter may make some amends —
Horace and we may yet be friends.'
   But Birrell just said 'Damn!'

Sir Edward Grey said, 'Birrell, come,
   Even you must surely think
We played it low on Plunkett.' Dumb
Was Birrell, only jerked his thumb
   Towards Ireland, with a wink.

Sir Edward Grey he shook his head
   And asked, with heavy sigh,
'Now that we have the letter read —?'
'Waste-paper basket,' Birrell said,
   And winked the other eye!

Ode to Bluff

O Heavenly Bluff descend on us,
God that each Ulsterman inspires,
Wake unto speech each timid cuss,
And make us sounding liars.
Arm thou the very economic man,
So without risk to life or limb he can
Fight battles greater far than Waterloo.
Grant him such stratagem as put to flight
The enemy who never came in sight.
Give talk of all that desperate men may do —
Such words as fall
From Carson's hallowed lips.
Give to us all
More fire, more earthquake, more eclipse,
But still take care that the last ditch be near
The first fence, over which our men may disappear.

Make us thy lyres even as Carson is.
Let us lay down our lives as he lays his.
Roll the dead multitudes before our words,
For we might cut ourselves if we drew swords.
But, Mighty-Mouthèd Bluff,
Warn us, thy slaves, when we have said enough.
Let us draw in our horns
At the right hour.
Grant us this power.
Suffer no man to tread upon our corns.
Give us the courage that can run away,
And let us live to bluff another day.

O thou on whom we place our sole reliance,
Who hast preserved us for a hundred years,
Even when we most had meditated fleeing,
And made our noisy tears
Seem moments in the being
Of an eternal defiance,
Hear us, Great Bluff!
O hearkener to the loud-clapping cheers,
The snorts of rage when we were safe enough,
Now let us pull the long bow with a yell,
A long pull and a short pull all together;
One that will frighten all our foes to hell
In this calm season of pre-Home Rule weather,
And make them see us weltering through their gore
And feel our mighty boots squash on them evermore.

Behold the Ulster boy,
His mother's darling joy!
Hear the dear child blaspheme
When Home Rule is the theme,
Between each tender kiss
Taught at the Pope to hiss.
This child, who blusters all he can,
Is father to the rampant Ulster man,
And we should wish our years to be
Bound each to each in such impiety.
With such good stuff our victory is sure;
With Craig, with Londonderry and with Moore
And Carson at their head,
Redmond and Devlin are as good as dead.
But if in spite of the loud Orange drum
Home rule should come,
Ulster will be in flight,
And Ulster will be right.

Susan Mitchell

The Voice Of One

Dramatis Personae - Bates, Barton, and M'Clure

BATES

I'd rather scrub floors on my marrow bones,
Throw chairs at mayors, or fling the Ogham stones
At English Kings' processions in hot weather,
Than hear your players playing plays together.

BARTON

'Tis true, the modern play is awful rot;
'Tis true, the theatre is gone to pot.

M'CLURE

I in fine raiment fain would clothe my skin,
But yet I toil not, neither do I spin.
I left Egyptian flesh-pots in a hurry,
Bearing with fortitude all kinds of worry,
Because I knew that surely somehow I
Might thrust a finger into some one's pie.
It doesn't matter whose the pie, or where —
Where'er the pudding is, M'Clure is there.
My metaphors to you, I know, are clear;
I'll reform everything, that's why I'm here.
I see the first thing is to cleanse the stage,
And — with your brains — to do it I'll engage.

BARTON

M'Clure, as far as all your friends can gather,
You don't wash well, although you raise a lather.

BATES

Look here, M'Clure, I'll wash my hands of you —
That's all the washing you and I will do.

M'CLURE

Why, you amaze me, what is it I've done?
I who love all men, and would injure none!

BATES

You stole my plot. . .

BATES

. . .And faked up all my play.

BARTON

Don't fling the chair at me, I'll go away. *[Going.]*
It's very queer, I long to be of use,
But all my efforts only earn abuse.
'Tis true, for that I do not care a jot,
I'd rather be abused than be forgot.

The Dublin pagans have given me a show,
Now at the Romans I will have a go.
If these do not my overtures receive,
The Protestants I've still got up my sleeve.
And when about me no more's left to say
From 'Parnell's Island' I will sail away
To dreamy Brixton, there to end my days
With the respectability that pays. *[Exit.]*

BARTON

Good riddance; now then, Bates, we will forget
Old scores, and have an Irish drama yet.
I have the money and the player's art,
And simple things are dear unto my heart.

BATES *(animated)*

That's it, that's it, simplicity's the thing;
Art is choked up by over-furnishing.
To make life simple is my whole design—
I who spend years upon a single line,
Setting a letter here, a comma there—
Surely simplicity's my only care.

BARTON

No doubt, no doubt; the thing is this, we want
A theatre and all the usual plant.

BATES

The usual plant! that's just the very thing
We must avoid; no over-furnishing.
The play must tell just by mere force of Art—
This is a matter I have much at heart.

BARTON

You must have clothes and properties and that,
Or else you plays will fall completely flat.

BATES

Had I the heavens' embroidered clothes indeed,
My stage and actors would no others need.
But these gay clothes long since in rain did fall,
So I won't hear of any clothes at all.

BARTON

You mean accessories, properties, and such,
You will not have your actors dress too much?

BATES

The passionate pulse of life is beating slow,
The wizard lips of life are murmuring low.
I gaze upon wan Beauty's shaken hair,
Actors and clothes and—everything are there!

Susan Mitchell

BARTON

What do you mean? Why, Bates, you must be mad.
And will you wreck our drama for a fad?
Think you I will good money fling away
To make the British critic holiday?

BATES

You're sordid, Barton, vulgar, and that's worse.
Money I leave to publishers, of course.
Of gold and silver little do I know,
But to my plays the gabbling world shall go.

BARTON

Faith, and I think they'll go there without me,
I leave you to your spectral company.
[Exit in rage.]

BATES

The mouthing world has frothed itself away,
And left me with my little plans to play.
Ocean of thought, how strange your ebb and flow!
No plans had I one little hour ago.
Dull people have their places, and my friends
Are usèd by the gods for their great ends —
The thrifty gods, who will true genius guide
To oysters with most precious pearls inside.
So these vain babblers, with their talk of plays,

75

Suggest new thoughts wherewith I will amaze
The stale old world that to the play-house goes
To look at scenery and look at clothes.
I've had my dreams of clothes and scenery too,
But well I know that way lies nothing new.
No gaudy, pinchbeck theatre for me,
The after-dinner lounge of bourgeoisie.
I for my plays will find a simple hall;
My stage — Shall I have any stage at all?
'The world's a stage,' a well-known writer states.
It is well said — though Shakespeare isn't Bates!
I'll have no stage, then I'll no scenery need
(Article two of my dramatic creed),
My players' clothes I will have wan and plain —
Ah, I forgot, from clothes they must refrain.
A pious thought, and near to Nature's plan,
My theatre of the primaeval man!—
A thought I hold by one long gleaming tress,
A thought of delicate, dim loveliness.
The Drama of to-morrow draweth nigh,
I its inventor, its creator I.
No theatre, no scenery, no stage,
No clothes the roving fancy to engage,
No actors either, for their gestures rude
Break in upon the spirit's solitude.
And neither shall my plays have any lines —
The straitened word the wingèd thought confines.
No, I will cause that a new thing shall be,
Plays shall be played in wordless wizardry.
For I shall sit in any room apart,
Just sit, and sit, and gaze in my own heart.
And when I toss the dim locks of my hair,
Dramas are born in men's minds everywhere.
And when I wave my slender pearl-pale hand,

Tragedy glides dream-heavy through the land.
All the world o'er the uncommercial few,
Gathering in companies of one and two,
Sit humbly while the miracle is wrought
By the unresting ravens of my thought,
While the mob theatre's expensive cloth
Makes ever still more fat the murderous moth;
And dew-pale ladies gather lilies tall
To weave o'er my white brow Fame's coronal!

Enter a Friend carrying patterns of costumes
for BATES' *next play, 'The Shadowy Daughters'.*

FRIEND

I've got some beautiful materials. See,
Silks opalescent, yea, and cramoisie.
I've thought out some great colour harmonies,
And I am sure we shall our audience please.

BATES

Ah! I've a scheme how clothes may spoken be,
In coloured notes unto the psaltery.
Show me the stuffs. . .

Enter Manager of a theatre.

MANAGER

. . . I have just found a man
Who has for scenery a novel plan.

BATES *(eagerly)*

I have a theory of waves of light.
And chanted words — I thought of it to-night.
    [Pressing his hand to his forehead.]
To-night, to-night —my Vision! —Woe is me,
Drown me in age-long dreams, sackbut and psaltery!

[CURTAIN]

EPILOGUE

Barton from Drama's gone, up in the skies
He sits aloft while choirs sing litanies;
No female choristers' impassioned noise,
But anthems masculine from nice small boys.
M'Clure is with us still, our own M'Clure,
His constant farewells we can still endure.
Parting to our M'Clure's the sweetest sorrow,
Farewell to-day, farewell again to-morrow.
O Eminent Farewellist, turn about,
We love your linkèd sweetness long drawn out.
Write us no dramas—only with us stay;
M'Clure, you're twice as good as any play!
Deep in the Abbey poets' corner laid
Bates sleeps and dreams his plays are being played
To crowded audiences that laughed and cried,
As in those days ere good old Shakespeare died.
Alas! those cultured, crowded days are done,
The Abbey echoes but — the Voice of One!
Bates sleeps, but there's a Day of Judgement when
I'm pretty sure Our Bates will rise again.

Lines on a Threatened Imperial University

'Pat, here's your University, you've got it safe and sound,
Brogues off, presumptuous Leaguers, the place is holy
     ground;
For Norfolk and his gentlemen are sailing o'er the sea,
Bad luck to you for Leaguers, will ye go to —Trinity!"
The Juggernaut of Compromise is crushing Irish flat,
O shade of sainted Patrick, they've put English upon Pat;
In classic Cockney he'll be taught the precepts of the wise,
While far off in farthest Arran the last native speaker dies.
Oh no, we will not come to heel whoever cracks the whip
Nor turn our glorious Sword of Light into a farthing dip
To light the 'little corner' they dole with niggard hand,
Good God! we claim for Irish every foot of Irish land.
If the counties pay the piper, the counties call the tune,
Nor mandarins nor bishops shall feed us with a spoon;
We did not fight for fifty years our dream at last to sell,
To hail the speech that banished ours to Connaught or to hell.
They'll come here from Australia, from Canadian ice
     and snow,
We're told the Yankee Irish in thousands here will flow;
Oh the melancholy New Zealander may sit within our walls,
While the lordly dream of Ireland we had in ruin falls.
Three thousand years of Irish life in Gaelic speech was told,
And through that Gaelic speech alone our history may unfold.
We'll see what bastard culture an English college gives,
When you slight the holy speech in which the soul of Ireland
     lives.
The young heart of young Ireland won't be withered by old
     men,
The speech of its Immortal Youth has come to it again.

79

Love's Mendicant

What do I want of thee?
No gift of smile or tear
Nor casual company,
But in still speech to me
Only thy heart to hear.

Others contentedly
Go lonely here and there;
I cannot pass thee by,
Love's mendicant am I
Who meet thee everywhere.

No merchandise I make,
Thou mayst not give to me
The counterfeits they take.
I claim Him for Love's sake
The Hidden One in thee.

The Tryst

I come to you, blind, hunted creeping things,
    I come your way;
Though I had chosen sun-sweet air and wings
    And the blue day,
Now through the clinging darkness I must creep,
    Dim citizens, with you my tryst to keep.

I've had my soaring time, my long, light day.
    Shall I complain
If for a space I go a heavier way
    In bonds and pain?
The lords of life know neither high nor low,
    The heart of man by many a road must go.

Dora Sigerson Shorter
(1866 - 1918)

Dora Sigerson was born in Dublin. Her father was George Sigerson, professor of zoology at the National University and an editor and historian of Irish literature, and her mother wrote a little. She herself belonged to the same literary circle as Katharine Tynan. In 1895 she married an English literary critic, Clement Shorter, and moved to London, where she remained until her death.

Her themes remained relentlessly Irish and typical of the Celtic Twilight throughout her career. Although her use of material is generally unimaginative and lacking much personal dimension or originality, her selection of raw material is in itself very interesting. She had a closer knowledge of traditional lore than any of the other writers in this book, either gained from direct contact with oral storytellers or from the perusal of collections of folktale and legend, which probably would have been at her disposal in her father's library. Rather than drawing on the tried and tested store of Old Irish mythology, she mainly used legends and stories which, although extremely popular among the oral narrators of Ireland, were seldom used by Irish writers: several examples of these narratives are included in the selection presented here: e.g. "The White Witch", based on the legend known to folklorists as "The Old Woman and the Hare", "The Man Who Trod on Sleeping Grass", based on the legend of the same name, "The Fairy Changeling", "The Banshee" and so on.

The Fairy Changeling

Brian O'Byrne of Omah town
In his garden strode up and down;
He pulled his beard, and he beat his breast:
And this is his trouble and woe confessed:

"The good-folk came in the night, and they
Have stolen my bonny wean away;
Have put in his place a changeling,
A weashy, weakly, wizen thing!

"From the speckled hen nine eggs I stole,
And lighting a fire of a glowing coal,
I fried the shells, and I spilt the yolk:
But never a word the stranger spoke.

"A bar of metal I heated red
To frighten the fairy from its bed,
To put in the place of this fretting wean
My own bright beautiful boy again.

"But my wife had hidden it in her arms,
And cried 'For Shame!' on my fairy charms;
She sobs, with the strange child on her breast:
"I love the weak, wee babe the best!"

To Brian O'Byrne's, the tale to hear,
The neighbours came from far and near:
Outside his gate, in the long boreen,
They crossed themselves, and said between

Their muttered prayers, "He has no luck!
For sure the woman is fairy-struck,
To leave her child a fairy guest,
And love the weak, wee wean the best!"

The White Witch

Heaven help your home to-night,
M'Cormac, for I know
A white witch woman is your bride:
You married for your woe.

You thought her but a simple maid
That roamed the mountain-side;
She put the witch's glance on you,
And so became your bride.

But I have watched her close and long
And know her all too well;
I never churned before her glance
But evil luck befell.

Last week the cow beneath my hand
Gave out no milk at all;
I turned, and saw the pale-haired girl
Lean laughing by the wall.

"A little sup," she cried, "for me;
The day is hot and dry."
"Begone!" I said, "you witch's child,"
She laughed a loud goodbye.

And when the butter in the churn
Will never rise, I see
Beside the door the white witch girl
Has got her eyes on me.

At dawn to-day I met her out
Upon the mountain-side,
And all her slender finger-tips
Were each a crimson dyed.

Now I had gone to seek a lamb
The darkness sent astray:
Sore for a lamb the dawning winds
And sharp-beaked birds of prey.

But when I saw the white witch maid
With blood upon her gown,
I said, "I'm poorer by a lamb;
The witch has dragged it down."

And, "Why is this your hands so red
All in the early day?"
I seized her by the shoulder fair,
She pulled herself away.

"It is the raddle on my hands,
The raddle all so red,
For I have marked M'Cormac's sheep
And little lambs," she said.

"And what is this upon your mouth
And on your cheek so white?"
"Oh, it is but the berries' stain,"
She trembled in her fright.

"I swear it is no berries' stain,
Nor raddle all so red."
I laid my hands about her throat,
She shook me off, and fled.

I had not gone to follow her
A step upon the way,
When came I to my own lost lamb,
That dead and bloody lay.

"Come back," I cried, "you witch's child,
Come back and answer me."
But no maid on the mountain-side
Could ever my eyes see.

I looked into the glowing east,
I looked into the south,
But did not see the slim young witch,
With crimson on her mouth.

Now, though I looked both well and long,
And saw no woman there,
Out from the bushes by my side
There crept a snow-white hare.

With knife in hand I followed it
By ditch, by bog, by hill:
I said, "Your luck be in your feet,
For I shall do you ill."

I said, "Come, be you fox or hare,
Or be you mountain maid,
I'll cut the witch's heart from you,
For mischief you have made."

She laid her spells upon my path,
The brambles held and tore,
The pebbles slipped beneath my feet,
The briars wounded sore.

And then she vanished from my eyes
Beside M'Cormac's farm,
I ran to catch her in the house
And keep the man from harm.

She stood with him beside the fire,
And when she saw my knife,
She flung herself upon his breast
And prayed he'd save her life.

"The woman is a witch," I cried,
"So cast her off from you".
"She'll be my wife to-day," he said,
"Be careful what you do!"

"The woman is a witch," I said;
He laughed both loud and long:
She laid her arms about his neck,
Her laugh was like a song.

"The woman is a witch," he mocked,
And laughed both long and loud;
She bent her head upon his breast,
Her hair was like a cloud.

I said, "See blood upon her mouth
And on each finger-tip!"
He said, "I see a pretty maid,
A rose upon her lip."

He took her slender hand in his
To kiss the stain away—
Oh, well she cast her spell on him,
What could I do but pray?

"May Heaven guard your house to-night!"
I whisper as I go,
"For you have won a witch for bride,
And married for your woe."

The Man Who Trod on Sleeping Grass

In a field by Cahirconlish
    I stood on sleeping grass,
No cry I made to Heaven
    From my dumb lips would pass.

Three days, three nights I slumbered,
    And till I woke again
Those I have loved have sought me,
    And sorrowed all in vain.
My neighbours still upbraid me,
    And murmur as I pass,
"There goes a man enchanted.
    He trod on fairy grass."

My little ones around me,
    They claim my old caress,
I push them roughly from me
    With hands that cannot bless.

My wife upon my shoulder
    A bitter tear lets fall,
I turn away in anger
    And love her not at all.

For like a man surrounded,
    In some sun-haunted lane,
By countless wings that follow,
    A grey and stinging chain,

Around my head for ever
    I hear small voices speak
In tongues I cannot follow,
    I know not what they seek.

I raise my hands to find them
    When autumn winds go by,
And see between my fingers
    A broken summer fly.

I raise my hands to hold them
    When winter days are near,
And clasp a falling snowflake
    That breaks into a tear.

And ever follows laughter
    That echoes through my heart,
From some delights forgotten
    Where once I had a part.

What love comes, half-remembered,
    In half-forgotten bliss?
Who lay upon my bosom,
    And had no human kiss?

Where is the land I loved in?
    What music did I sing
That left my ears enchanted
    Inside the fairy ring?

I see my neighbours shudder,
    And whisper as I pass:
"Three nights the fairies stole him;
    He trod on sleeping grass."

Goodbye

And so goodbye, my love, my dear, and so goodbye,
E'en thus from my sad heart go hence, depart;
I cast thee out, renounce, and hold no more;
I wreck the cup of joy thou heldest for drinking
To my lips, thinking we'd quaff—be as before;
Yet at my laughter if thou hearest sigh,
And ask no question "Why?"
Believing only that my pleasure lies
To find approval in thy pleasèd eyes.

Before our time, my dear, my dear, Fate so had planned
Our little race to run beneath the sun,
That we should meet and love and dream, then separate.
Perchance, she thought, though, there would be no parting,
No salt tears smarting; she deemed to mate
My most imperfect self to thine, and gain
A better harvesting of pain:
I weep, but null is Fate's decree—
Such tears fall not so bitterly.

I saw a woman once undo and then pursue
Old letters with hard eyes; through such disguise
I pierced and knew her weeping.
"And such he was," she said, "whose is the failing
That love is paling? which is the soul that's sleeping?"
His step; and quick the letters put in hiding:
They meet with cold eyes chiding.
If I were such as she,
Oh, death were well for me!

I saw a man's grey eyes fill up, and overfull
Let fall two sparkling tears, as one who fears;
Draw forth a curling braid of woman's hair,

Lay it across his lips with swift caressing,
His love confessing: "My sweet beyond compare,
Whose fault we love to-day and hate to-morrow?"
Her voice: he hides his sorrow,
And meets her bitterly;
And oh, if thou wert he!
I saw two children wondering, hand in hand,
Sit dumb beside their hearth, as if their mirth
Were stricken by some fear past understanding;
Find in their parents' eyes with silent reading
The old degrading truth beyond commanding —
The bond of love that held two hates united,
They plead still unrequited,
They grow and bear the thorn-
Oh, better never born!

Better if thou wert dead, my dear, if thou wert dead;
No woman's moan but mine should hush thy sleeping.
When other eyes should close, their watch forgetting,
My vain regretting still their watch was keeping;
When other hearts grew weary by death's gates,
Stole to their loves and hates,
Mine still lived for its laughter
In what might come hereafter.

Goodbye! I would not have thee dead. We grasped at stars
That only God could take: we tried to make
A paradise for keeping
Upon an earth where He had wrecked the garden;
Giving no pardon, baptized us all in weeping.
So pass; goodbye! Some other woman's love,
Oh! not as great as mine, will find above
Some happier fate to choose you
Than mine that did refuse you.

All Souls' Night

*[There is a superstition in some parts of Ireland that the dead are
allowed to return to earth on the 2nd of November (All Souls' Night)
and the peasantry leave food and fire for their comfort, and set a chair
by the hearth for their resting before they themselves retire to bed.]*

O mother, mother, I swept the hearth, I set his chair
    and the white board spread,
I prayed for his coming to our kind Lady when Death's
    sad doors would let out the dead;
A strange wind rattled the window-pane, and down the
    lane a dog howled on.
I called his name and the candle flame burnt dim, pressed
    a hand the door-latch upon.
Deelish! Deelish! my woe forever that I could not sever
    coward flesh from fear.
I called his name and the pale Ghost came; but I was
    afraid to meet my dear.

O mother, mother, in tears I checked the sad hours past
    of the year that's o'er,
Till by God's grace I might see his face and hear the
    sound of his voice once more;
The chair I set from the cold and wet, he took when he
    came from unknown skies
Of the Land of the Dead, on my bent brown head I felt
    the reproach of his saddened eyes;
I closed my lids on my heart's desire, crouched by the
    fire, my voice was dumb.
At my clean-swept hearth he had no mirth, and at my
    table he broke no crumb.
Deelish! Deelish! my woe forever that I could not sever
    coward flesh from fear.
His chair put aside when the young cock cried, and I
    was afraid to meet my dear.

Ethna Carbery
(1866 - 1902)

Ethna Carbery was the pseudonym of Anna Isabel Johnston. She was born in Ballymena, Co Antrim and lived most of her life in Belfast. She married the Donegal writer, Seamus MacManus in 1901, and she died in 1902.

More interested in the Nationalist political movement than any of the other poets included in this volume, she edited the magazine *Shan Van Vocht*, with Alice Milligan, from 1896 to 1899, and contributed verse to it and to other patriotic magazines. She did not publish a collection of poems during her life, but a few collections were published posthumously and proved very popular.

Her poems consist largely of love poems, with an emphasis on loss and unrequited love. She makes some use of mythology and also wrote ballad-type poems celebrating the exploits of Ulster heroes such as Niall O'Cahan and Red Hugh O'Donnell. It is one of these heroic songs, Roddy MacCorley, for which she is best remembered.

Love of Donegal was one of her abiding passions and her best poems are those which are concerned with nature — something which she has in common with most of the poets in this collection. Carbery never writes purely nature lyrics, however: they are always adulterated by some patriotic or mythological concern, and, while her obvious visual sensitivity and fascination with colour render some of her poems attractive, little she wrote rises above the conventional. It is possible that, had she lived longer, she would have improved.

Ethna Carbery

Consummation

In a sheltered, cool, green place
You and I once stood together,
Where the quickens interlace.

Then it was our love declared
(Thro' a throstle's silver chiming)
All the passion that it dared.

Then you called me by my name,
And the answering eyes I lifted
Flashed a flame unto a flame.

Hushed, we watched the eve descend
The rose-flecked stair of day, to see
Our heart's probation fitly end.

Stars and mist and dew-wet flowers
Scented, shielded, and made holy,
That sweet hour of the hours.

Oh Dear Heart, life holds no gift
Half so precious, half so brittle,
As this Love-cup that we lift.

*And remembering, down the years
All my songs shall echo sighing,
All my laughter trill with tears.*

A Glen Song

There's a green glen in Éirinn,
A green glen in Éirinn!
Do you remember yet, *a gradh*, the sunshine of that day,
How the river ran before us, and the fleckless blue hung
    o'er us,
And against the purple heather gleamed the yellow of
    the hay?

There's a green glen in Éirinn,
A green glen in Éirinn!
Where on a dew-wet swinging spray brown throstles
    trilled above,
And the blackbird carolled after in a silver rain of
    laughter,
And the little linnet piped its song that has no theme
    but Love.

There's a green glen in Éirinn,
A green glen in Éirinn!
'Twas sweet with you beside me in a world of harvest
    gold;
The sallaghs made a shadow in a corner of the meadow,
And your eyes were wells of kindness, and my hand lay
in your hold.

There's a green glen in Éirinn,
A green glen in Éirinn!
The voice of Spring comes on the winds like cuckoo
    calling clear,
She bids us fare together, nor heed the fitful weather—
And seek in yon green glen the joy that waits our hearts,
    my Dear.

Rody M'Corley

Ho! see the fleet-foot hosts of men
Who speed with faces wan,
From farmstead and from fisher's cot
Upon the banks of Bann!
They come with vengeance in their eyes—
Too late, too late are they—
For Rody M'Corley goes to die
On the Bridge of Toome to-day.

Oh Ireland, Mother Ireland,
You love them still the best,
The fearless brave who fighting fall
Upon your hapless breast;
But never a one of all your dead
More bravely fell in fray,
Than he who marches to his fate
On the Bridge of Toome to-day.

Up the narrow street he stepped,
Smiling and proud and young;
About the hemp-rope on his neck
The golden ringlets clung.
There's never a tear in the blue, blue eyes,
Both glad and bright are they—
As Rody M'Corley goes to die
On the Bridge of Toome to-day.

Ah! when he last stepped up that street,
His shining pike in hand,
Behind him marched in grim array
A stalwart earnest band!
For Antrim town! for Antrim town!

He led them to the fray—
And Rody M'Corley goes to die
On the Bridge of Toome to-day.

The grey coat and its sash of green
Were brave and stainless then;
A banner flashed beneath the sun
Over the marching men—
The coat hath many a rent this noon,
The sash is torn away,
And Rody M'Corley goes to die
On the Bridge of Toome to-day.

Oh, how his pike flashed to the sun!
Then found a foeman's heart!
Through furious fight, and heavy odds,
He bore a true man's part;
And many a red-coat bit the dust
Before his keen pike-play—
But Rody M'Corley goes to die
On the Bridge of Toome to-day.

Because he loved the Motherland,
Because he loved the Green,
He goes to meet the martyr's fate
With proud and joyous mien,
True to the last, true to the last,
He treads the upward way—
Young Rody M'Corley goes to die
On the Bridge of Toome to-day.

The Other

I am the Other—I who come
    To heal the wound she gave,
The wound that struck your fond words dumb,
    And left your world a grave.

What though you loved her—I love you,
    And so the most is said,
Here is my yearning heart, still true
    To yours her frailty bled.

(But oh! the bitter grief that I
    Kept hushed, the wild despair,
When your dear eyes had passed me by,
    To find her face so fair.)

Now she hath gone her cruel way,
    And I am come again,
To seek among the husks to-day
    For one sweet golden grain.

Because in me Love's strength is great,
    Too great for pride, or sin,
I knock upon your heart's barred gate,
    And pray you let me in.

The Love-Talker

I met the Love-Talker one eve in the glen,
He was handsomer than any of our handsome young men,
His eyes were blacker than the sloe, his voice sweeter far
Than the crooning of old Kevin's pipes beyond in Coolnagar.

I was bound for the milking with a heart fair and free —
My grief! my grief! that bitter hour drained the life from me;
I thought him human lover, though his lips on mine were cold,
And the breath of death blew keen on me within his hold.

I know not what way he came, no shadow fell behind,
But all the sighing rushes swayed beneath a fairy wind;
The thrush ceased its singing, a mist crept about,
We two clung together-with the world shut out.

Beyond the ghostly mist I could hear my cattle low,
The little cow from Ballina, clean as driven snow,
The dun cow from Kerry, the roan from Inisheer,
Oh, pitiful their calling — and his whispers in my ear!

His eyes were a fire; his words were a snare;
I cried my mother's name, but no help was there;
I made the blessed Sign — then he gave a dreary moan,
A wisp of cloud went floating by, and I stood alone.

Running ever thro' my head is an old-time rune —
"Who meets the Love-Talker must weave her shroud soon."
My mother's face is furrowed with the salt tears that fall,
But the kind eyes of my father are the saddest sight of all.

I have spun the fleecy lint and now my wheel is still,
The linen length is woven for my shroud fine and chill,
I shall stretch me on the bed where a happy maid I lay —
Pray for the soul of Máire Og at dawning of the day!

Eva Gore-Booth
(1870 - 1926)

Eva Gore-Booth was born at Lissadell, Co Sligo, the younger sister of the more famous Constance, later Countess Markievicz. She spent most of her adult life in Manchester, where she lived with the suffragette, Esther Roper, probably in a lesbian relationship. She was herself involved in social work, socialist politics and in women's issues.

Although her verse dramas, such as "Unseen Kings", were heavily influenced by the Celtic Twilight style of writing, many of Gore-Booth's poems, from the earliest to the last, are quite independent of this influence and indeed do not seem to fit easily into any school of Irish writing. Her use of language and form may be conventional and seldom striking, but it is sturdy, generally unpretentious (which is very unusual) and often classically elegant; her mastery of formal poetics is complete. Her range of theme and subject matter are wide-ranging, unusual, and independent: she had a truly exploratory sensibility and intelligence, and her poems reveal her own philosophical and intellectual journey through life. Less overtly emotional than the other poets whose work is included in this volume, she seems to me to have a more vigorous and questioning mind than any of them;her mastery of formal poetics is complete. Her concern with the politics of the women's and workers' movements are unusual; her poems about the First World War are strong and original; her interest in the condition of the artist and the role of art is more or less unique, at least among Irish women poets.

Of the poets whose work is presented here, Eva Gore-Booth is she whose poems come closest to belonging to the modernist movement, and whose mind seems clearest and untrammelled by pernicious sentimentality. Her poems are intellectual rather than sensual, in this differing radically from most of the others in this book, but paying a price for that.

A Nightmare

I WROTE eight verses late last night,
And slept, and lo! a wondrous sight,
There came eight funerals instead
Marching slowly past my bed.
As they went each nodding plume
Swayed and rhymed across the gloom.
    In the twinkling of an eye,
The whole procession passed me by,
And every verse—became a hearse
    To carry murdered poetry.

After the Storm

SUDDENLY everywhere
    Clouds and waves are one,
The storm has cleared the air,
    The sea holds the sun
And the blue sky —
    There is no under, no above,
All is light, all is love —
    Is it like this when you die?

The Weaver

I WAS the child that passed long hours away
Chopping red beetroot in the hay-piled barn;
Now must I spend the wind-blown April day
Minding great looms and tying knots in yarn.

Once long ago I tramped through rain and slush
In brown waves breaking up the stubborn soil,
I wove and wove the twilight's purple hush
To fold about the furrowed heart of toil.

Strange fires and frosts burnt out the seasons' dross,
I watched slow Powers the woven cloth reveal,
While God stood counting out His gain and loss,
And Day and Night pushed on the heavy wheel.

Held close against the breast of living Powers
A little pulse, yet near the heart of strife,
I followed the slow plough for hours and hours
Minding through sun and shower the loom of life.

The big winds, harsh and clear and strong and salt,
Blew through my soul and all the world rang true,
In all things born I knew no stain or fault,
My heart was soft to every flower that grew.

The cabbages in my small garden patch
Were rooted in the earth's heart; wings unseen
Throbbed in the silence under the dark thatch,
And brave birds sang long ere the boughs were green.

Once did I labour at the living stuff
That holds the fire, the water and the wind;
Now do I weave the garments coarse and rough
That some vain men have made for vain mankind.

The Land to a Landlord

YOU hug to your soul a handful of dust,
And you think the round world your sacred trust —
But the sun shines, and the wind blows,
And nobody cares and nobody knows.

O the bracken waves and the foxgloves flame,
And none of them ever has heard your name —
Near and dear is the curlew's cry,
You are merely a stranger passing by.

Sheer up through the shadows the mountain towers
And dreams wander free in this world of ours, —
Though you may turn the grass to gold,
The twilight has left you out in the cold.

Though you are king of the rose and the wheat,
Not for you, not for you is the bog-myrtle sweet,
Though you are lord of the long grass,
The hemlock bows not her head as you pass.

The poppies would flutter amongst the corn
Even if you had never been born,
With your will or without your will
The ragweed can wander over the hill.

Down there in the bog where the plovers call
You are but an outcast after all,
Over your head the sky gleams blue —
Not a cloud or a star belongs to you.

The Little Waves of Breffny

THE grand road from the mountain goes shining to the sea,
And there is traffic in it and many a horse and cart,
But the little roads of Cloonagh are dearer far to me,
And the little roads of Cloonagh go rambling through my
    heart.

A great storm from the ocean goes shouting o'er the hill,
And there is glory in it and terror on the wind,
But the haunted air of twilight is very strange and still,
And the little winds of twilight are dearer to my mind.

The great waves of the Atlantic sweep storming on their way,
Shining green and silver with the hidden herring shoal,
But the Little Waves of Breffny have drenched my heart
    in spray,
And the Little Waves of Breffny go stumbling through
    my soul.

The Street Orator

At Clitheroe from the Market Square
    I saw rose-lit the mountain's gleam,
I stood before the people there
    And spake as in a dream.

At Oldham of the many mills
    The weavers are of gentle mind;
At Haslingden one flouted me,
    At Burnley all the folk were kind,

At Ashton town the rain came down,
    The east wind pierced us through and through,
But over little Clitheroe
    The sky was bright and blue.

At Clitheroe through the sunset hour
    My soul was very far away:
I saw Ben Bulben's rose and fire
    Shining afar o'er Sligo Bay.

At Clitheroe round the Market Square
    The hills go up, the hills go down,
Just as they used to go about
    A mountain-guarded Irish town.

Oh, I have friends in Haslingden,
    And many a friend in Hyde,
But 'tis at little Clitheroe
    That I would fain abide.

Women's Trades on The Embankment

"Have Patience !"—The Prime Minister to the Women's Franchise Deputation, 19th May 1906.

WHERE the Egyptian pillar —old, so old —
    With mystery fronts the open English sky,
Bearing the yoke of those who heap up gold,
    The sad-eyed workers pass in silence by.

Heavily hewing wood and drawing water,
    These have been patient since the world began —
Patient through centuries of toil and slaughter,
    For Patience is the ultimate soul of man.

Patient with endless lords and overseers,
    Since long-dead Israelites made bricks to please
A King whose heart was hardened to their tears,
    What time they still besought him on their knees.

Their patience was the King's confederate,
    Their weakness helped his power unaware;
In vain men pray unto the rich and great,
    For only God-like spirits answer prayer.

Long has submission played a traitor's part —
    Oh human soul, no patience any more
Shall break your wings and harden Pharaoh's heart,
    And keep you lingering on the Red Sea shore.

The Romance of Maeve

THE harvest is scant, and the labourer,
Returning at sunset with so few sheaves,
Has gathered gold bracken and silver fir
And boughs of the elm and the brown beech leaves.

Fuel enough for the evening blaze,
When the blue of the sky grows wintry and pale,
And the pilgrim home from the wild wood ways
Can read by the fire an ancient tale:

How great Queen could cast away her crown,
The tumult of her high victorious pride,
To rest among the scattered fir-cones brown
And watch deep waters through the moon-light glide.

The Anti-Suffragist

THE princess in her world-old tower pined
A prisoner, brazen-caged, without a gleam
Of sunlight, or a windowful of wind;
She lived but in a long lamp-lighted dream.

They brought her forth at last when she was old;
The sunlight on her blanchèd hair was shed
Too late to turn its silver into gold.
"Ah, shield me from this brazen glare!" she said.

Roger Casement

I DREAM of one who is dead,
As the forms of green trees float and fall in the water,
The dreams float and fall in my mind.

I dream of him wandering in a far land,
I dream of him bringing hope to the hopeless,
I dream of him bringing light to the blind.

I dream of him hearing the voice,
The bitter cry of Kathleen Ni Houlighaun
On the salt Atlantic wind.

I dream of the hatred of men,
Their lies against him who knew nothing of lying,
Nor was there fear in his mind.

I dream of our hopes and fears,
The long bitter struggle of the broken-hearted,
With hearts that were poisoned and hard.

I dream of the peace in his soul,
And the early morning hush on the grave of a hero
In the desolate prison yard.

I dream of the death that he died,
For the sake of God and Kathleen ni Houlighaun,
Yea, for Love and the Voice on the Wind.

I dream of one who is dead.
Above dreams that float and fall in the water
A new star shines in my mind.

The Artist in War Time

Oh, shining splendour of the human form
That takes my heart by storm,
Strong as a river, subtle as a prayer,
Or the first moon ray in the twilight air,
Line upon line of moving silver light,
Building our dreams up to the spirit's height,
Enfolding the grey dust and the earth's green
In coloured ecstasies of light unseen!
The Spirit that moves among the forest trees
Has doubtless built this shrine,
That erring men may fall upon their knees
And worship God and man, one soul divine—
Yea, and the little children of the earth
That make the world sweet with their wanderings,
And wild -willed pilgrims of mysterious birth
Gliding across the sky on silent wings.
Ah, surely no man born dare rise and slay
Eternal Beauty wrapped in robes of clay,
Or break and blast and utterly destroy
Life's little ivory tower of fragile joy!
Loud answerèd the black and stupid guns,
"We are the darlings of man's heart, the wise
Call us the world's Redeemers, mighty ones
Have bid us clear for them the troubled skies,
And holy souls have blessed us, for we stand
For God Almighty in a godless land.
God, Who art feeble grown and blind and dumb,
Take heart, through us Thy Kingdom yet shall come."
Labourers in mad mechanic purpose bound,
They did in vain Immortal Beauty's grave,
And bury the very starlight underground,
And crash above the song of wind and wave

Their monstrous rhythms of fire and steel and lead.
On some red field or battle-blasted hill
Men dream the Eternal Beauty lieth dead,
And all our souls are subject to their will.
Most ancient Beauty, scorned and thrust aside,
Who doth yet in white peace and silence dwell,
Pity us tortured slaves of bloodstained pride,
Lean out once more from the invisible,
Let fall from thy dream-haunted obscure throne
One ray of moonlight in earth's broken brain.
Our souls are thine, Belovèd, thine alone,
Behold thy lost world at thy feet again.

The World's Grief

"IN all earthly happenings
Claws are better far than wings —
Force has dug the grave of Love,"
Said the Tiger to the Dove.

"A little venom on the tongue
Beats any song that e're was sung —
Great are lies and shall prevail,"
Said the Snake to the Nightingale.

"Always with the great pack fight,
For the pack is always right —
Oh, be loyal if you can,"
Said the Wolf unto the Man.

"For every good under the sun
Man must fight with sword and gun —
Woe to the gentle and the mild,"
Said Man to the human Child.

"In the war of right and wrong
The victory is to the strong —
Great guns must clear your darkened sky,"
Said Man to the Lord Most High.

The moon turned pale, the stars stood still.
"Peace upon earth, to men good will,"
The Angel to the Shepherd cried.
Christ turned in His sleep and sighed.

Dreams

THE swallows flit through twisted branches fine
And silver arches of the bare plane trees,
Where scant stiff leaves sway in the passing breeze,
Clinging to dreams of May, green robed, divine.

Alas ! our dreams are only of the dread
Red fields of France where unreaped harvests rot,
And the One Soul by all the world forgot
Moves silently amid the hosts of dead.

German or French or English, words most vain
To that which knows not any nation's pride,
Whose pity is as all men's sorrow wide,
Folded about our broken world of pain.

Knowing no foe in any death or life,
Moving in dreams in every darkened mind,
Whilst still to death the blind lead on the blind,
That comradeship is deeper than our strife.

Men drench the green earth and defile her streams
With blood, and blast her very fields and hills
With the mechanic iron of their wills,
Yet in her sad heart still the spirit dreams.

True to all life, war-worn and battle tossed
Doth the One Spirit, faithful to the end,
Live in that peace that shall be the world's friend,
The dream of God by men so lightly lost.

To C. A.

YOU seem to be a women of the world,
Gorgeous in silky robes of blue and green,
Hair in soft shining coils, white throat bepearled.
It is not true, you are what you have been.

I know you for the Umbrian monk you are,
Brother of Francis and the sun and rain,
Brother of every silver pilgrim star,
And the white oxen on the golden plain.

Where one bird's song the evening silence thrills
To beauty, white your mountain convent gleams,
Brown-robed, barefoot, across the Tuscan hills
I see you wander, smiling at your dreams,

Stopping to help a peasant at his toil,
Gathering the olives, watering the vine,
Guiding the plough, turning the red-brown soil,
Sharing the evening meal of bread and wine,

And passing on your way at the day's end
To sleep on the pine-shadowed, leaf-strewn sod,
Fearlessly finding all the world your friend,
And living in the Beauty that is God.

The Little Girl's Riddle

A JELLY-FISH afloat on the bright wave—
A white seagull — a great blue butterfly —
A hunted hare — a wolf in a dark cave;
All these I was; which one of these was I?

A gold-maned lion, mad with rage and fear,
A white bear ranging over trackless snow,
A savage living by my bow and spear,
A mighty fighter giving blow for blow,

A student gazing at the starry skies,
A Rebel planning the downfall of Kings,
A searcher of the wisdom of the wise,
A questioner of all mysterious things,

A priestess singing hymns to Proserpine,
And old king weary on a golden throne,
A marble-carver freeing limbs divine
From their cold bondage of enfolding stone,

A hot-head poet by the world reviled,
A heretic of desolate dreams and dire,
And now a little silent long-legged child
Weeping alone beside the nursery fire.

Ye who have guessed the hidden lights that burn
Behind the blue wings of the butterfly,
In a child's grief the riddle's answer learn —
"I was all these—yet none of these was I."

An Experience

I LABOURED and studied and toiled and thought,
And it all came to nought —
My thoughts and my mind and my soul seemed dead
As the books that I read —
When suddenly a little door,
Hidden far down in the deeps of consciousness,
Swung open, and a ray of light
Flooded each dim recess.
I left myself's safe shore
And swam across the night.
Deep down beyond life's overthrow
Where only the reckless care to go,
I caught a glimpse of a star divine,
That changed the lights and shadows of all things
With rays as swift as a seagull's wings.
And for a moment brief
As the flash and fall of a leaf,
A yellow leaf on a hurrying stream,
I saw strange meanings shift and change and gleam,
As if some new enraptured hope
Had shaken life's kaleidoscope
To patterns little understood,
Beyond the evil and the good —
It may have been a dream
But it was not dead
Like the books I read,
And the labour and the toil and the pain
Seemed suddenly worth while,
If I might see and understand again
Life's strange and secret smile.
Shall my sad heart be prisoned evermore
In a dark cave behind a barrèd door?

The Poet to His Ambition

O VANITY, who diggest in my soul
For those lost words and splendid, go thy ways,
Take with thee thy shrill trumpet, thy bright scroll,
I will not sell my life for any praise.

Behold another digger sighing stands
Beside me, she shall have thy spade.
Dear Love who digs for Truth with humble hands,
All Life and Light are thine, come to my aid.

A Dweller by the Ocean

OH very near the wide Atlantic shore
Is my white cottage homestead dark and low,
No idea neighbours stand about the door,
But great waves storming past the window go.

At times I dream the Atlantic infinite
Watching the sun rise over fields of foam,
And smile to think those floods of gracious light
Flow round the darkness of my narrow home.

When light fades from the green-lit fields of surf,
Wave shadows flicker on the white-washed wall,
I stir to flame the smouldering heap of turf,
And dream of greatness in my cottage small.

Then the wind moans athwart the unquiet sea,
Thin streaks of white across the ocean creep,
And, in my soul, forgotten ecstasy
Stirs restlessly and shudders in her sleep.

But when the bitter storm wind lifts and shakes
My little cottage, least of fragile things,
Out of the deeps of memory awakes
The soul's voice weeping o'er her broken wings.

Again the lost divine procession fair
Crosses the humble threshold of my mind;
A rush of wings makes pure the evening air,
And the dark hour gives sight unto the blind.

Then is the veil of woven fancy rent,
Into the eyes of truth again I gaze,
And read the doom of the long banishment,
My soul shrinks backward from the lightning's blaze.

Not pure enough for vision, and not just
Enough for justice, yet too pure and wise
To be thus lightly mingled with the dust,
And look at earth and sea with clay-built eyes.

Yea, the poor soul, the sorry charioteer,
By wings uplifted, by desire undone,
Seems to my heart that God dethroned and dear
Who yet was Lord of the far-shining sun.

Oh, fallen majesty, austere, unseen,
So weak and captive, easy to forget,
My heart gives homage to the Veilèd Queen,
Phoebus among the herds is Phoebus yet.

I who eat porridge from a wooden bowl,
Whilst one dim candle gutters in the gloom,
Do wonder at the greatness of the soul,
And narrow windows of the little room.

The Elm Boughs

THE Elm boughs shudder in the sooty wind,
From their bright leaves the City children know
That somewhere the black world is glad and kind,
And through green woods the sunlit breezes blow.

All starved and stunted from the poisoned sod,
They shiver upwards through the stainèd air;
These are the battered pioneers of God,
Waving His green flag in the city square.

Thus in the grey-built city of the mind
Wave the green boughs of a few hostage powers,
Their secret whispered to the soilèd wind
Hold all our faith in Beauty's austere flowers.

Somewhere the fair and secret troops of Spring
Shine in strange colours icy clear and cold,
But I pass on through dark streets wandering,
Or dream a dream beneath the elm boughs old.

The Human Adventure

ON these wave-haunted sands the children play,
And silver twilight, clad in radiant gleams,
Comes laughing down the hill from Knocknarea,
With a gay company of wandering dreams.

The while a dog in careless ecstasy,
Trusting the guidance of a human hand,
Plunges forth headlong into the wild sea,
Brings but a stick and courage back to land.

So in the incarnation of the Wise
At times it seems a light and foolish whim
To brave the abyss for such a doubtful prize,
Plunged in wild waters of the twilight dim.

Yea, the tired spirit struggling with the tide
Of flowing life and monstrous waves of time,
Clutches but feebly her immortal pride,
And clings unto a broken bough of rhyme.

When the strong swimmer rescued from the wave,
Deep in the sunlight grass enraptured lies,
May she hold fast the secret of the grave,
The light of Peril in her dauntless eyes.

Nora Hopper Chesson
(1871-1906)

Nora Hopper Chesson's father was Irish, but she herself was born in Exeter and lived all her short life in England, mainly in London. She is regarded, however, as the "quintessentially Celtic Twilight" poet, and was heavily influenced by Yeats and Katharine Tynan, both of whom she occasionally plagiarized.

Her first volume of poems, *Ballads in Prose*, was published when she was twenty-three, and several more collections followed. While her subject matter is always highly romantic and fantastical, with fairies, winds, and drowned girls abounding, her use of language and imagery is appealing. Like many of the poets in this volume, she had a strong sense of colour and the visual, and the warm golden tones which colour many of her poems render them immediately attractive. She is at her best in her simpler nature lyrics and a few samples of these have been included. On the whole she is rather a cheerful poet, and there is an optimistic celebratory note in most of her work which is unusual and not unwelcome.

Soontree

(A Lullaby)

My joy and my grief, go sleep and gather
Dreams from the tree where the dreams hang low,
Rounder than apples, and sweeter than honey,
All to delight you, ma creevin cno!

My joy, fill your dear hands full of roses,
And gather lilies that stand a-row:
Pull rush and reed with the Shee's fair children,
But eat not, drink not, ma creevin cno!

You may not taste of the cups of honey,
You may not taste of the wine blood-red,
Of the mead and the wine he drank, your father,
And the next night's rain wept your father, dead.

Reach up to the star that hangs the lowest,
Tread down the drift of the apple-blow,
Ride your ragweed horse to the Isle of Nobles,
But the Shee's wine drink not, ma creevin cno!
    Shoheen, shoheen, shoheen sho!

The Dinny Math

(To W. B. Y.)

We are the gentle people:
    The passing dust we are,
With gusty laughter blowing
    Near and far.
We are the gentle people,
    Nor deal in praise or blame,
But we stand before your sorrow,
    And we stand behind your shame.

We are the gentle people,
And soft our music's blown
When kindly hearts that loved us
Are passing from their own.
We are the gentle people,
And gently draw away
The light feet to our dancing
Night and day.

We are the gentle people,
    And though our toll we take
Of milk and meal and water—
    For old sake's sake
Ye grudge us not, who grudge not
    To watch your folded kine,
To bless the wheels and the pillows
    And the lace-threads fine.

We are the gentle people,
    Mavrone, and we shall pass
Even as the dew, that Morning
    Dries from the short green grass.
Oh, the dew returns at twilight,
    But not so we —
We shall pass like wind, so be ye kind
    To the passing Shee.

Gold Song

"Gold of butterflies, gold of bees,
Gold of ragweeds and golden seas;
Gold on gorses for kissing's sake,
Which of these will you touch and take,
      Moirín, Moirín?"

Golden butterfly's not for me,
I'll ha' none o' the golden bee:
My heart of gold shall not beat nor break,
Though I love the gorses for kissing's sake,
      Mother, Mother!

"Then rest you merry, through heat and cold,
Sweet lips of cherry, sweet heart of gold;
Yet Gold-Heart surely shall come some day
To cry for gray wings to fly away,
      Moirín, Moirín!"

Wild Geese

Wild Geese, wild Geese, where are you going?
The mist's before you, behind's the rain:
The red east wind thro' your plumes is blowing —
When will it blow you back home again?

Wild Geese, wild Geese, where you are going
My heart goes also, and fain would flee —
Farther away where the Hunter's glowing,
But Miscann Many's the light for me.

After the wildfire I must follow,
Tho' the way is dark where I set my feet —
While you fly hence amid crying hollow,
The wind's long keen, and the lash of sleet.

Good speed, wild Geese, and a truce to sighing!
Fair fall your way over wind and wave,
Till I awaken, and hear you flying
Over and over my bogland grave.

Ceol-Sidhe

There never was any music
In the golden throat of a bird,
More fine and clear than the piping
That in dreams I heard
Cry through the Heart Lake's rushes,
And falter and fade away,
Like odours of thyme one crushes
    In the heat of the day.

There never was any piping
So sweet and tender and gay,
It came like the wind, and lightly
    It blew away —
It laughed and it grew not weary,
It sighed and was sweeter yet,
It sang for the hope of Eri
    And her heavy fret.

There never was any piping
So merry and none so sad,
For it sang of a far green island
    Where, scarlet-clad,
All under the druid quicken,
Wild dancers gather and go,
And under the oaks, unstricken,
    Feeds Saav, the doe.

And when silence took the piping,
"It's O to be there," I cried,
"To dance with no thought of grieving
    For joy that died —
To dance, and never be weary

For night or day,
With the kindliest folk of Eri
   Till the dew's away.
Sweet, sweet is the twilight dancing,
Not sweet is the homespun day."
But the dawn through the rushes glancing
   Drove my dream away.

A Song of Four Winds

The gray wind out of the West
    Is sighing and making moan,
For a noinin's silver crest
    In the hay-swathes overthrown.
Like the heart in a dying breast,
    It flutters, making its moan,
The gray wind out of the West.

The black wind out of the North
    Blows loud, like a cry of war:
Its voice goes gallantly forth
    In fields where the spearsmen are:
To them is its voice not worth
    Wild music of any star?
The black wind out of the North.

The white wind out of the South,
    It makes not for war nor peace:
'Tis the breath of a colleen's mouth,
    Yet it flutters the willow-trees:
It burns men's souls with drouth,
    Then fills their souls with ease:
The white wind out of the South.

The red wind out of the East —
    What word can a harper say
Of the wind that blows from the feast,
    And blows men into the fray:
It will not stay for the priest,
    For the Host it will not stay —
The red wind blowing out of the East,
    The wind of the Judgement Day.

A Drowned Girl to Her Lover

I hear the hill-winds, I hear them calling
The long gray twilights and white morns thro',
The tides are rising, the tides are falling,
And how will I answer or come to you?
For over my head the waves are brawling
And I shall never come back to you!

Dark water's flowing my dark head over,
And where's the charm that shall bid it back?
Wild merrows sing, and strange fishes hover
Above my bed o' the pale sea-wrack:
And Achill sands have not kept for my lover
The fading print of my footstep's track.

Under the sea all my nights are lonely,
Wanting a song that I used to hear.
I dream and I wake and I listen only
For the sound of your footfall kind and dear,
Avourneen deelish, your Moirin's lonely
And is the day of our meeting near?

The hill-winds coming, the hill-winds going,
I send my voice on their wings to you, —
To you, ma bouchal, whose boat is blowing
Out where the green sea meets the blue:
Come down to me now, for there's no knowing
But the bed I lie in might yet hold two!

The Short Cut to Rosses

By the short cut to Rosses a fairy girl I met;
I was taken in her beauty as a fish is in a net.
The fern uncurled to look at her, so very fair was she,
With her hair as bright as seaweed new-drawn from out
    the sea.

By the short cut to Rosses ('twas on the first of May)
I heard the fairies piping, and they piped my heart away;
They piped till I was mad with joy, but when I was alone
I found my heart was piped away and in my breast a stone.

By the short cut to Rosses 't is I'll go never more,
Lest I be robbed of soul by her that stole my heart before,
Lest she take my soul and crush it like a dead leaf in her hand,
For the short cut to Rosses is the way to Fairyland.

Brigit of The Judgements

I am Brigit — Wisdom, Light: yea, I am Bride.
I loosen all the knots that wrong has tied;
I knot all threads that should be woven in one.
I am the giver of laws; all evil done
Is on my heart until I may unravel
Its web with heavy tears and bitter travail.
My hair is coloured like the heather honey;
My brows are cloudy and my eyes are sunny.
Judgement I hold in one hand, in the other
Pity; I am both maiden and a mother.

I am the judgement-giver; but I give
Compassion to all burdened things that live,
Struggle, and prey, and so are preyed upon.
Because the work-girl's hollow cheeks are wan,
Mine are so pale. Because the red ant dies
Under a careless foot my deathless eyes
Are dark with dool. Because the red fox went
Snarling to death, the lilies have no scent
That are amid my breast-knots tied, to show
I am the mother of all that fade and grow.

One man may call me Wisdom who has heard
Some darkling midnight stabbed through with my word.
One man will call me Light who, ere he dies,
Grasps at my hand and looks me in the eyes.
I am no Lianan-sidhe; I will not follow
The soul that seeks me even in the hollow
Lands where the moon is not or any sun,
No travail ended and no quest begun.
I slay the man who called me Law and strove
To slay me, but one name of mine is Love.

Weed-Fires

Now every little garden holds a haze
That tells of longer nights and shorter days:
Handfuls of weeds and outcast garden-folk
Yield up their lives and pass away in smoke.
The leaves of dandelions, deeply notched,
Burn with the thistle's purple plumes, unwatched
Of any eyes that loved them yesterday,
And flare in sullen flames, and pass away.

The small fires whimper softly as they burn;
They murmur at the hand that will not turn
Back on the dial and bring to them again
June's turquoise skies or April's diamond rain.
"Alas," the weeds are crying as they smoulder,
"We are grown wiser with our growing older;
We know what summer is — but ah! we buy
Knowledge too dear; we know because we die."

In Kew Gardens

The lake is blue, the lake is gray.
Around the lake tall flag-leaves sway
And swither in the gentle wind.
The sun is strong enough to blind
Weak eyes that love a shaded room.
The tulips break in scarlet bloom.
Blood-red, wine red, the peonies stand
Like purpled flames on either hand.

The peacocks spread their splendid fans
And flaunt before the pelicans.
Wisht doves in yonder elm-trees try
To mock the cuckoo's wandering cry
With drawling voices sad and soft,
Half lost among the leaves aloft.
The white moth with the brown moth flies
In shadowy silken companies.

Blue into amber fades away;
The furthest trees are hazy gray;
The purple clouds grow tender green;
The rosy clouds mass soft between.
The wild-fowl by the water-side
Cry as if man's first day had died
And Adam, naked, stood alone
'Neath the first darkness he had known.

Sources

Katharine Tynan
Ballads and Lyrics, London, Kegan Paul, 1891.
A Lover's Breastknot, London, Elkin Mathews, 1896.
Innocencies, London, Bullen/Dublin, Maunsell, 1905.
Experiences, London, Bullen, 1908.
New Poems, London, Sidgwick and Jackson, 1911.
Irish Poems, London, Sidgwick and Jackson, 1913.
The Holy War, London, Sidgwick and Jackson, 1926.
Late Songs, London, Sidgwick and Jackson, 1917.
Collected Poems, London, Macmillan, 1930.

Susan Mitchell
*Aids to the Immortality of Certain Persons Living in Ireland,
     Charitably Administered*, Dublin, Maunsell, 1912.
The Living Chalice, Dublin, Maunsell, 1913.

Dora Sigerson Shorter
The Fairy Changeling, London, Lane, 1898.
Collected Poems, London, Hodder and Stoughton, 1908.
Love of Ireland, Dublin, Maunsell, 1916.

Ethna Carbery
The Four Winds of Erin, Dublin, Gill and Macmillan, 1934.

Eva Gore-Booth
Poems of Eva Gore-Booth, London, Longmans,
Green and Co., 1929.

Nora Hopper Chesson
Under Quicken Boughs, London, John Lane, 1896.
Selected Poems, Edited by W. H. Chesson, London, Rivers,
1906.